D1603037

A Catholic Woman's
Guide to Romance

A CATHOLIC WOMAN'S GUIDE TO ROMANCE

Rose Sweet

TAN Books
Charlotte, North Carolina

Cover design by Caroline K. Green

Cover image: Old wooden door with bougainvillea in Cyprus. Photo by dinosmichail/Shutterstock.

Library of Congress Control Number: 2019930530

ISBN: 978-1-5051-1224-5

Published in the United States by
TAN Books
PO Box 410487
Charlotte, NC 28241
www.TANBooks.com

Printed in the United States of America

Contents

PART I

About Romance

To fall in love with God is the greatest romance; to seek him, the greatest adventure; to find him, the greatest human achievement.

—St. Augustine of Hippo

Our world has "magic" doorways

Like Dorothy's farmhouse door, mysterious openings to the interior world are all around us. They are not magic as in sorcery or New Age, but natural entryways that lead to the mysterious and supernatural world that coexists with ours. God has secrets, but because he loves us, he wants us to discover them. Some doorways are natural—like nature, music, art, or science—and others are supernatural, like prayer and the sacraments. They all lead to the same transcendent realm from which we came and to which we are destined to return: the very heart of God.

Living in Kansas, Dorothy was restless—something inside her was calling. Life on the farm with Uncle Henry and Auntie Em just wasn't cutting it. She wanted deeper meaning, a greater happiness, and was willing to leave the safety and familiarity of home for a grand adventure. Have you been restless and longed to go farther, deeper, and higher than ever? From childhood, I believed romance was my great destiny; despite its thrills and pleasures, I discovered it was only a doorway to something greater.

Romance, and all the wild, passionate longings that come with it, is one of those natural gateways that will take us to God—if we let it.

Are you ready for an adventure into the interior life? Here are some things to remember before we leave the farm.

The turbulence of life can take us to magical places

In a sense, Dorothy Gale's story is prophetic; it is often the ominous storms of life and the terrible tornadoes of suffering that yank us violently out of our self-focused, black-and-white lives to discover something more profound. I never really noticed the hidden passages in this life that lead to ultimate happiness. I was too busy in my own little world to see God's mysteries and hear his voice. So if you ever get stuck in that restless place, I say let the clouds appear and the wind begin to blow!

Doorways are all around us

Once we have the eyes to see, we will discover that doorways to the interior life are all around us. God is calling you into the interior world.

He invites you to enjoy the gifts he has bestowed upon you in this world but always to let them serve as signs to lead you deeper. In fact, his call is less of a summons than it is a proposal for the ultimate happily-ever-after romance. After all, adventure and romance go hand-in-hand!

"God, infinitely perfect and blessed in himself, in a plan of sheer goodness freely created man to make him share in his own blessed life. For this reason, *at every time and in every place*, God draws close to man. He calls man to seek him, to know him, to love him with all his strength" (CCC 1, emphasis added).

Romance is a secret way of seeing into heaven

At its heart, everything that is romantic is a clue to seeing God as *the Bridegroom who deeply longs for you, his beloved Bride.* The saints and mystics know that romance is the beginning of what is called "bridal spirituality," one of many ways to understand God's love for us and our relationship with him.

Authentic spirituality is not about communing with nature, experiencing deep emotions, stretching, breathing, or lowering your stress level—although those can be results of it. Rather, it's about really seeing and being drawn closer to God, a Person who desires loving, life-giving union with you. Through the colorful world of this "spousal imagery," I trust you will be surprised and delighted to see or remember that:

- his words of love are ever-present,
- traces of his divine presence are everywhere,
- and his love notes are written on everything he created.

Here are some other things to think about.

The pure of heart will see this imagery first

It's embarrassing to admit that we can't see something someone else can. We've all been given the eyes to see beyond this visible world, but sadly, we've become too distracted, jaded, or are afraid to let go of the safe, secure world we've created for ourselves. Jesus said we must be like little children, wide open to the wonders he has for us.

You have to really want to see the unseen

Do you believe in fantasy? By itself, it can seem to be merely man-made myth, but with God's grace, you *can* see past the poetry to the fullness of truth. Fantasy reveals man's desire to see and enter the supernatural world—which we as Catholics know is real.

Contrary to a popular cultural belief that you can visualize something and make it happen, simply wanting to see something will not get it for you. Trust me; I've visualized the same ten pounds (okay, fifteen) gone a million times! But with God's grace and a guide to help you on your journey, you will be able to truly see the mystical.

God wants to wow you!

As a child (and even still today), I was so excited to see Munchkin Land, the enchanted forest, and then the breathtaking brilliant-green grandeur of the Emerald City. Oz is a doorway to the deeper understanding that there truly is a place "no eye has seen, . . . no ear has heard, and . . . no human mind has conceived" all the things God has prepared for those who love him (see 1

Cor 2:9). Remember, just because you don't see something doesn't mean it's not there. You just need to walk through the door.

Reflections

- Have you ever seen or sensed something supernatural?
- Do you prefer life to be straightforward or mysterious? Why?
- Do you have a memory of some beautiful doorway? Where was it?

2

Expanding the Definition

*Romance is the glamour which turns the
dust of everyday life into a golden haze.*

—Elinor Glyn, *The Philosophy of Love*[2]

I went on my first romantic date when I was
seven.

Being the oldest child, I often got to stay up
later than my younger siblings. One night, I was
in my blue flannel pajamas watching TV with
my Dad. Suddenly, he got an urge for a chocolate milkshake, and when he discovered there
was no ice cream in the house, he decided to run
out for a treat.

---

[2]   Elinor Glyn, *The Philosophy of Love* (Whitefish,
MT: Kessinger Publishing, 2010).

"Honey," he hollered to my mother. "I'm going out to get a chocolate shake. Can I bring you one back?" Mom said yes and to please add extra malt.

"I'm taking Rosie with me," he added.

"But Daddy, I'm in my pj's!"

Dad smiled and grabbed his car keys.

"Put on your shoes and a coat, Rosie-Posie. No one will ever know!" He grinned.

I won't forget how special I felt that night. I got to sit in the front seat of the car where Mom usually sat. Inside the restaurant, we drank our milkshakes while he asked me about my schoolwork. It's been over sixty years, and every time I am back in Sacramento, I drive by the old commercial neighborhood on El Camino Avenue—now a run-down industrial area. The dilapidated building was still there last time I visited. Someday it will be demolished, but my first-date memories will always stand.

Life is one big romance

Let's start with a greater cosmic meaning of romance: *it is the expression and/or experience of love through beauty.* Any passionate knitting of minds, hearts, and souls through what is lovely can be, in a sense, "romantic" and need not be sexually motivated. Just as God can romance us with the splendor and delights of this world, other people can "romance" us with love that is sweet and pure. Romance is expressing love through beautiful words and gestures.

My friend Allison Gingras was introduced to Brother Simon, CFR (Franciscan Friars of the Renewal), at a Catholic tradeshow. Upon meeting him, she knew she would be expected to go through the customary ritual of extending and shaking hands. It's a very personal bodily contact with a stranger when you think about it, and Allison shared what happened. "I did what I have had to do in that circumstance for the last three years. I recoiled my hand and apologized for the severe eczema that had caused numerous red, itchy blisters all over my hands and fingers. It's what I call my hand leprosy, making a joke about needing a sign that says 'unclean.' But to my utter amazement, he took my hand and kissed it. Touching my heart so deeply, his kiss cracked open my hard-hearted nature and I burst into tears."

We are all made for safe, warm, loving communion with others. We're made for what I call little marriages, to be wooed by and unite ourselves forever with something good, true, and beautiful.

- As children we sometimes want to "marry" our parents.
- We soon begin to express loyal, 'til-death-do-us-part emotional attachment to our playmates.
- Little girls often make vows to grow old together and raise their future families in side-by-side cottages with front porches and rocking chairs.
- We can swear oaths of love and friendship, trade rings or bracelets, and—as my brothers used to do—even become "blood brothers."
- We even recognize this intense level of friendship between men as a "bromance."

Romance reflects and draws us to God

Romantic notions are often expressed in a wide variety of ways. Sometimes we say a person has "fallen in love" with her hobby, is "married" to the job, or that the golf course is his "mistress." In a sense, we are all destined for some sort of "marriage"; that is, being completely committed and united to something we deeply desire and perceive as good.

Art or music can *romance* you into a pleasurable union with beauty.

A sales clerk can *seduce* you with the promise of a pleasurable purchase.

Your employer can *woo* you with the promise of a profitable partnership.

A lover can *court* his sweetheart into marriage.

All of these are clues, helping to point to God's universal and supreme wooing of the soul into an eternal life-giving union.

Romance plays on our desires, draws us through our senses, and leads to the *One* who is *True, Good*, and *Beautiful*—the classic "Four Transcendentals." These four are attributes of God, and they are the highest objects of human thought and contemplation. At the same time, however, you can never reach the end of them; they are inexhaustible mysteries that surpass our capacity to understand them in their fullness. There is no limit to the depths of truth, the riches of goodness, or the endless forms of beauty—all the things we desire.

In many ways, an encounter with the True, Good, and Beautiful compares to the experience of falling in love and becoming, as C. S. Lewis observed, "love's contemplative."

> Very often what comes first is simply a delighted pre-occupation with the Beloved—a general, unspecified pre-occupation with her in her totality. A man in this state really hasn't leisure to think of sex. He is too busy thinking of a person. The fact that she is a woman is far less important than the fact that she is herself. He is full of desire, but the desire may not be sexually toned. If you asked him what he wanted, the true reply

would often be, "To go on thinking of her." He is love's contemplative.[3]

Romance is a path—through beautiful words, gestures, and things—that is meant to point to and lead us to God.

Our mind needs the fullness of Truth.

Our soul needs authentic Goodness.

Our heart needs genuine Beauty.

Beauty invites us into truth

Goodness and beauty will lead us to the truth of who we are. One of my nieces, Marissa, shared what she sees as "momentary romance" versus "lifestyle romance." She believes that romance shouldn't be reserved for a couple's anniversary dinner but should be the basis of a life that draws anyone into what is true, good, and beautiful. I agree! You don't have to be wealthy to appreciate and enjoy the romance of life. You can:

- enter intentionally into the *beauty or drama of nature* (roaring fire,

---

[3]   C. S. Lewis, *The Four Loves* (New York: Harcourt Brace, 1960).

bright spring day, rain, moonlit night),

- experience and savor *times of change and mystery* (autumn leaves, first snow, shadows, sunsets, twinkling lights, candlelight, liturgical seasons),
- experience and remember *good smells* (cigars, pipes, perfumes, soap, pine, wood burning, freshly-turned earth, flowers, fresh-baked bread, church incense),
- be part of the hustle and bustle of *city pleasures* (museums, restaurants, bars),
- use, enjoy, or give *beautiful things* (china, crystal, lace, fur, silver, gold, paper, wood),
- listen to *beautiful music* (slow, poignant, peaceful, passionate, joyous, chant),
- share or listen to *poetic readings* (stories, letters, expressions of love, Scripture),
- prepare or share *good food*,

- share and enjoy *intoxicating drink* (aged, fine, mellow, sparkling),
- or experience *delightful touch* (water, warm, soft, cool, cozy, fluffy, snuggled, smooth, sleek, gentle, firm handshakes, bear hugs, kisses, pats, hand-holding, blessings).

Reflections

- What is your first romantic memory?
- What do you think is a most romantic gesture?
- What type of music says "romance" to you?

3

Exploring the Erotic

Affection is taken as the image when God is represented as our Father; Eros, when Christ is represented as the Bridegroom of the Church.

—C. S. Lewis, *The Four Loves*[4]

"**O**h-h-h, is this for me? Why, *thank you!*"
The first person who ever brought me flowers was a boy named John who gave me a wrist corsage for the El Camino High School freshman homecoming dance. His blonde hair was slicked down with Brylcreem, he smelled like English Leather cologne, and he nervously handed me the clear plastic box that contained a single beribboned carnation. I was thrilled—I'd

---

[4]   C. S. Lewis, *The Four Loves* (New York: Harcourt Brace, 1960).

never seen flowers tinted with blue dye to match my dress! Of course, as we get older, we graduate to much more sophisticated (and expensive!) blooms, like lilies, orchids, or long-stemmed roses.

Flowers from a friend are lovely, but when they come from someone of the opposite sex who is interested in romance, they have a much different meaning. They promise a different kind of love, and they often stir up a different kind of response. John's floral gift was nice . . . but let's face it, I wanted him to give me my first kiss!

Traditional romance leads to eros

Romance is about love, but love is complicated—no one will argue that. John never did kiss me, but the dreaming of and hoping for it was almost as sweet as kisses that came a few years later from Terry at junior prom. The ancient Greeks came up with terms for what we call today the four classic types of love.

> Philia – warm and tender platonic love between friends

The bonds here do not need to be strong to be good.

Storge – natural, accepting love between family members
This love has deeper natural bonds than mere friendship.

Eros – love for one person that delights in the senses and often stirs sexual passions.
Without agape, this love can disintegrate into self-centered pleasure.

Agape – highest form of unconditional, self-sacrificing love
This is the love we all want, the most unselfish, and the kind we are supposed to have for even our enemies. You don't have to feel friendship, family bonds, or erotic attraction to love this way. Agape starts in the will.

Erotic love needs agape love

With our parents, friends, and family, we can all enjoy the "romance" of life. Traditionally, though, we tend to equate romance with eros—sexual attraction and desire. The true meaning of *eros* is a bit different than our modern term *erotic*, which we often associate with thoughts or actions that are naughty and sinful.

Originally, *eros* described the healthy common expressions of physical love. In the Scriptures, *eros* primarily refers to those passionate expressions between a husband and wife. The Bible does not shy away from the reality of romantic love—nor even from the sexual pleasures of married love. Indeed, the Scriptures elevate it to a sharing in the love that God has for man—as evidenced in the erotic and romantic love poetry of the Song of Solomon.

In this romantic poem, the couple experience all the ups and downs, intense longings of wanting to be together, and being "sick with love" until they can be together. Here the Bride is extolling the attributes of her Bridegroom and longing for the sweet taste of his kisses—and more!

> O that you would kiss me with the
>   kisses of your mouth!
> For your love is better than wine,
>   your anointing oils are fragrant,
> your name is oil poured out; there-
>   fore, the maidens love you.
> Draw me after you, let us make
>   haste. (Sg 1:2–4)

The handsome Bridegroom extolls her beauty—her eyes, her smell, her lips. He is beguiled by her!

> You have ravished my heart, my
>   sister, my bride,
> you have ravished my heart with a
>   glance of your eyes,
> with one jewel of your necklace.
> How sweet is your love, my sister,
>   my bride!
> how much better is your love than
>   wine,
> and the fragrance of your oils than
>   any spice!

>Your lips distil nectar, my bride;
>honey and milk are under your tongue;
>the scent of your garments is like the scent of Lebanon. (Sg 4:9–11)

He praises her beautiful body and wants to delight in her all night long!

>Your two breasts are like two fawns,
>twins of a gazelle,
>that feed among the lilies.
>Until the day breathes
>and the shadows flee,
>I will hasten to the mountain of myrrh
>and the hill of frankincense. (Sg 4:5–6)

She's ready! She wants her feminine scents to allure him into her "garden of delights" and all the juicy, rich, sweet love she has to offer him.

>Awake, O north wind,
>and come, O south wind!

> Blow upon my garden,
>   let its fragrance be wafted
>   abroad.
> Let my beloved come to his garden,
>   and eat its choicest fruits. (Sg
>   4:16)

In our "pornified" world, many cannot read this without being scandalized. But when the mind and heart are purified, we see in this bridal imagery a reflection of God's sweet longing for each of us—and his desire that we open to let him enter our hearts. In that, we see, too, that agape is fulfilled in the wild and rightly-ordered passion of eros.

Romance draws us in with beauty

In the first of his many famous sermons on the Song of Solomon, Saint Bernard of Clairvaux aptly describes marriage as "the sacrament of endless union with God." *Romance is an invitation—through beautiful words, gestures, or created things—that leads to life-giving communion.* It includes all good desires to possess (and be possessed by), consume (and be consumed by), and be perfectly united with something good. In bridal theology, that something good is God—the Ultimate Good.

In the Song of Solomon, notice the sensory descriptors and the comparison with delicious food and wine: *See me! Smell me! Hear me! Touch me! Taste me!* And even *eat and drink me*! Traditional romance either leads with or leads to eros (all that delights the senses), but to endure—and bring us to the fulfillment of our deepest desires—it must also include genuine friendship, a familial bonding, and be rooted in self-sacrificing agape love.

That is the true romance that lasts.

Reflections

- Who were you first passionately attracted to? How old were you?
- Did you ever experience feelings of wanting to be completely consumed by love?
- Who gave you your first memorable kiss? Is the memory pleasurable, painful, or both?

4

Going to the Cross

*As coroner I must aver, I thorough-
ly examined her. And she's not only merely dead; she's really most sincerely dead!*

—Munchkin Coroner, *Wizard of Oz*[5]

In the movie *The Wizard of Oz*, Dorothy is bored and blind to the underlying beauty, truth, and goodness of the Midwest prairies, her family, and her farmhand friends. Seeking happiness elsewhere, she is transported to another realm full of color, mystery, and even love, but she ultimately longs to return home. When she does, though, she is changed. At the end of her

---

[5]   *The Wizard of Oz*, motion picture, screenplay by Noel Langley.

wild adventure through Oz, Glenda, the Good Witch, asks her what she has learned.

Dorothy wistfully replies, "That if I ever go looking for my heart's desire again, I won't look any further than my own backyard, because if it isn't there, I never really lost it to begin with."

Oh, how right she is! The truth about *our* hearts' desires—happiness, love, and romance—has always been ours within the teachings and wisdom of the Catholic Church. But to some, the Church seems as dry and parched as a Kansas plain. We always seem to be looking for something more colorful, more entertaining, somewhere "over the rainbow." Blind to the truth—as I once was—I hope those who are lured away from our Church will wake up and see; perhaps when a little dog pulls back the curtain to reveal the doddering old imposter. And the truth is this: real romance and true love always lead to the cross. This is the heart of our faith.

In Dorothy's story, her "happily ever after" could only come when she chose to leave the childlike world of Munchkins, go into the unknown, face danger, and even risk her life for the greater good of those she loved. Real romance is not about seeking the glitter of the Emerald City via the yellow brick road, but by seeking the shining gold city on the hill by the way of the cross.

Real romance embraces the cross

Charlie is in his sixties, with grey hair and decades of memories, but he recalls the first time he felt romantic.

"I was four years old and almost ready for kindergarten. I thought Dad was bigger than life. I used to watch him shave, and I really wanted to be a man like him. I also wanted to be a hero like Roy Rogers and the Lone Ranger.

"And, man, I thought Mom was so beautiful. I can even remember the smell of her perfume. Maybe it was seeing how Dad loved her, and how she loved him in return—they never shied away from kissing in front of us kids—but I also wanted to love her and be *her* hero.

"One morning, Mom was outside planting rose bushes in the brick planter around our house. The older kids had gone off to school and there was no one to help her. So I looked at the potted plants Mom had brought home from the nursery and decided I would pick one up and carry it over to her. It was so heavy that I could hardly carry it. And—son of a &@##%—it had sharp thorns that poked into my chest and actually drew blood! All these years later, I still never forget how much it hurt, but I didn't want to be a wimp, and I really wanted to make Mom happy, so I carried it all the way over to her and said, 'Here, Mom,' and I put that damn plant down."

I laughed.

"Do you remember what she said to you?"

"Oh, yeah. Like it was yesterday. She smiled and thanked me and told me she loved me. That I was her little man. I felt so proud."

Charlie's romantic feelings moved him to express love that was not just sentimental—as in giving his mother flowers. Instead he went to where romance should lead: through authentic, self-giving sacrifice.

Charlie is my brother.

Our mother *was* beautiful, and Dad *was* our hero. Our parents encouraged all of us nine little Sweets to read adventure and romance stories and watch them on television and in the movies, and these stories shaped how we saw the world and ourselves in it. More accurately, though, they reflected and drew out the romance that was already in our hearts. And we learned that real romance leads to true love—love that's forged in sacrifice.

Romance should lead to true love

Enjoying the pleasures of romance without moving to some form of life-giving communion between hearts would be to indulge only in sentimental feelings that can mislead. Think back: how many men have courted you with gifts, flowers, wine, music, and promises of love only to lead you on or leave you? Was there a cross they were avoiding? Sentiment is sweet, but without authentic, sacrificial love it can be nauseating.

True love must be tested over time

In the Garden of Eden, Adam and Eve were "romanced" by the enemy—through the sensual delight of a "fruit"—and bought into all his empty promises. Thus, their trust in God and each other was lost, perfect love was corrupted, and the "holy communion" they enjoyed with God and each other was defiled. Love that endures must be tested by the heavy crosses of rejection, danger, or death; otherwise it is weak, crumples, and blows away in the first strong wind. In the overcoming of *error, evil, and ugliness*, love grows strong roots and bears sweet, fragrant flowers and rich, delicious fruit: *unity, truth, goodness, and beauty.*

Some forty years after Charlie sacrificed himself for our mother, she was tragically overcome by dementia. Mom would not eat, bathe, or take care of herself, and she desperately needed medical attention. Daily she lashed out in confusion and anger at our father who was himself elderly and struggling to care for her. So we four older siblings gathered together and arranged to get mom into a medical facility. As tenderly and lovingly as we planned to pull it off, we knew we would run into resistance.

Charlie took the lead.

"Calling an ambulance or medical team will only frighten Mom. We need to get her there ourselves. She's physically weak. After you girls explain to her what is happening and where we are taking her, I'll pick her up and carry her to the car and hold her until we get there. You guys get in and then, Barb, you drive."

Mom did not want to leave her safe spot on the sofa where for a few years she had been sleeping, eating, and surrounding herself with hundreds of little yellow Post-it notes to help her remember things.

She was confused and scared, and when we told her we were taking her to get help, she shut down. Charlie had to gently but firmly pick her up, hold her tightly to his chest, and carry her out of the house. With her weak and feeble fists, she tried to pound his chest and cried, "Where are you taking me? Put me down, put me down. *I hate you!*"

We arrived at the hospital where caring professionals assured, calmed, and tended to her. Eventually she was released into a good senior care facility where we would visit her regularly. We discovered she also had a form of leukemia, and she died a few short years later.

With tears in his eyes, Charlie told me later,

"Rose, that day was the hardest thing I've ever done. When she tried to hit me and throw out her barbed comments, my chest remembered the piercing pain of the rose bush. But just like I did back then, I had to take the hit. I was doing this for Mom because I loved her."

Remember, Prince Charming did not come only to slay a dragon and brag to his friends afterward over a beer. That would merely reduce him to a pest exterminator. No, he killed the monster to free and become one with what he saw as the ultimate source of happiness and goodness: his Beloved. Embracing the cross crushes fear, selfishness, and sin to release true love into the universe.

G. K. Chesterton said, "The true soldier fights not because he hates what is in front of him, but because he loves what is behind him."[6]

---

[6]   G. K. Chesterton, *Illustrated London News*, January 14, 1911, in the *Collected Works of G. K. Chesterton*, vol. 29.

Reflections

- Can you recall a time you freely chose to suffer for someone out of love?
- What is your favorite romantic movie and why?
- Did you ever see one of your parents sacrifice out of love for the other?

5

Ruling the Heart

Do not be afraid, then, when love makes demands.
Do not be afraid when love requires sacrifices.

—Pope St. John Paul II[7]

M y first little love affair didn't end well.

I was five, Terry lived next door, and a redwood fence separated our suburban neighborhood lots. One day while I was playing in our backyard, I heard Terry's voice beckoning to me.

"Rosie, come over here!"

"Where?" I called back. I was delighted that my cute young neighbor wanted to talk to me, but the fence was high, and I was short.

---

[7]   Pope John Paul II, Pastoral Visit in New Zealand, *Address of John Paul II to the Young People, Auckland (New Zealand), Domain Park, 22 November 1986.*

"Over here!"

I followed his voice.

"There's a hole in the fence. Look in it!"

I found a large knothole and pressed my little face up against the rough, splintery wood.

Just then, Terry poked a sharpened pencil through the hole and stabbed me in the cheek. I heard him and his brother, Ricky, laughing hysterically. I was shocked! Thankfully, it missed my eyeball and hit my bone socket, but I ran, crying and clutching my bloody face, into the house.

"Mama-a-a!

I was never allowed to play with Terry again.

Romance has rules

That was just the beginning of my dreams for love that ended in some unhappy situations— including a memorable date with Jim.

Jim was tall and rugged, with strawberry blonde hair and a cleft chin. He was smart, funny, and all of our mutual friends found him to be congenial and engaging. Our conversations were stimulating, and I loved that he could make me laugh so easily. We had started dating, and after a few times out to dinner, I began to notice something I didn't like: he always flirted with the waitresses.

He wasn't just being "friendly" but really oozing the charm, holding her gaze a little longer than necessary, and laughing a little too exuberantly at her cute comments. Not wanting to appear jealous or insecure, I brushed it off at first. *It's just his "salesman" personality*, I told myself. *Be glad he's not a stick in the mud*, I added.

But it kept happening, along with his ogling any exceptionally beautiful woman who was also passing by. One night, while I was trying to share something important over the dinner table, I saw his eyes follow our waitress down the aisle and over to the bar area.

I was not happy.

"Um, *excuse me*, I'm over here!" I said lightly and with a little smile. I was hoping he would get the point.

He laughed and seemed to understand. But just before dessert, he excused himself to go to the restroom and was gone a long time.

Don't look around. Stay cool, I thought. But I turned around anyway. There he was, standing at the waiter's station, close up and engaged in flirtatious conversation with our waitress.

I was upset, but all the relationship books I had ever read said not to confront but to explain—at the right time and place. So after dinner, when we were in the car headed home, I brought it up.

"Jim, thank you for a lovely dinner. It was great (*gulp*) except for one little thing. I love how outgoing you are with everyone, but sometimes feel that I have to compete with our waitress or other pretty women."

I paused and tried to add as gently as I could, "When I am out with a man, I hope that he will only have eyes for me!"

I smiled sweetly and batted my eyelashes, not quite knowing how he would take it and a bit afraid of conflict.

For the first time, he didn't know what to say and sat quietly for a moment.

He sighed, slightly nodded his head, and said, "Okay."

Success!

The next week he pulled up outside my house for another date. He got out of the car, opened my door to let me in, and then opened the car trunk and pulled something out. When he climbed back into his seat, he looked into the rearview mirror and put on a pair of eyeglasses, to the sides of which he had taped two large black squares of cardboard.

At first, I laughed.

"What are those?" I asked.

"They're blinders," he replied matter-of-factly.

"Blinders?"

"Yes."

Then he added, "Since I'm not *allowed* to look at other women, I figured I have to wear these when I'm with you."

Okay, at first it seemed pretty funny, and—I admit—pretty clever. I know humor can often help to lighten an uncomfortable subject. But there was a sarcastic edge to him, and he was passively and purposely putting me in my place.

Not nice.

I was young back then; if I could go back in time, I would immediately get out of the car, turn on my high heels, and advise him,

"Wake up, Buckwheat! Relationships have rules."

Rules protect love

No one likes to be told what to do, even when we know we should do it. We are all instinctively fearful that someone will control us or keep us from the pleasures we think we deserve.

When you are naïve, ignorant, and childish, you only see rules as restrictions on your freedom and fun.

With wisdom and maturity, you see that rules provide the structure and safety for authentic freedom and fun.

Rules are safeguards against disorder and even danger. In our fallen world, anything good needs the protection that rules provide. Romance has rules, some of which include:

- Thou shalt be patient and kind.
- Thou shalt open the door for others.
- Thou shalt wait thy turn and let others go first.
- Thou shalt make sure thy spouse or date or friend has a drink.
- Thou shalt listen attentively to what others are saying.

- Thou shalt see, appreciate, and express the goodness of others.
- Thou shalt not hog the conversation.
- Thou shalt not take the biggest piece for thyself.
- Thou shalt not be rude, crude, or arrogant.
- Thou shalt not shame or bully others.
- Thou shalt not flirt on a date with others.

Are these heavy burdens to be imposed upon you or are they simply the natural desires of the heart when you love someone? *Think about it:*

- When the heart is full of *self*, it needs the rules.
- When the heart is full of *love*, it does not need the rules.

Relationships have rules because true love has demands . . . to seek and uphold the True, Good, and Beautiful and avoid the lies, evil, and ugliness that can creep into it.

Reflections

- Did a love interest ever treat you badly?
- Have you ever been rude or selfish to a boy-friend or spouse?
- What is one thing you will not tolerate from a love interest?

6

Speaking in Rituals

We lack rituals in this modern world.

—Elizabeth McGovern (Cora
in *Downton Abbey*)[8]

In my marriage retreats, I have a lot of fun asking couples what they did to prepare for their first date. The women immediately start chattering, and their conversation is lively as they share things like:

- Went to the mall and tried new lipsticks

---

[8] Carol Memmott, "A regal return – to a new world – for 'Downton Abbey,'" *USA Today*, Jan. 2, 2013, https://www.usatoday.com/story/life/tv/2013/01/02/downton-abbey-returns-fellowes/1791829/.

- Spent hours trying on new jeans
- Bought a whole new outfit
- Got a facial or a makeover
- Purchased new shoes
- Cut their hair or got a new style
- Bought a new perfume
- Spent money on costly body lotion
- Borrowed or bought earrings or other jewelry
- Invited friends over to help pick the outfit
- Went to Pinterest for more ideas
- Read magazine articles for helpful tips
- Tried to lose ten pounds in three days
- Went to the tanning bed
- Had their eyebrows tweezed
- Had other body hair waxes
- Shaved their legs for the first time in a long time . . .

When I ask the men what they did, they look around at each other in awkward silence.

Finally, one will speak up: "I washed the car."

Everyone laughs, but then we have a frank

discussion about the rites and rituals of romance. It's not that men don't prepare, but they tend to do it differently. One of our universal feminine gifts is to bring beauty into the world, so we often spend more time on that. A man's universal gift is to provide and protect, so we sometimes forget all that they do:

- Wash and clean out the inside of the car
- Vacuum it and cover up the coffee stains
- Buy or use air freshener
- Stock spare change in the console for parking meters
- Make sure the gas tank is full
- Check the air in the tires
- Put breath mints in the glove box
- Call the restaurant and make reservations
- Make sure they get a good table
- Go to the bank and get cash
- Check their wallet for the AAA card
- Make sure they have all their credit cards (paid down)

- Take a shower
- Put on fresh socks
- Wear clean clothes

These men are going through the timeless rituals of preparing for love so that we women are well taken care of. Yes, I know, we gals can do all those things they do, but isn't it nice to have someone plan ahead and take care of us? Yes, it is!

If you find yourself insulted by, or fearful or resentful of manly provision, it's probably because in past experience you have been used or hurt. Maybe someone taught you to distrust men. Ask God for help to heal so that your feminine heart can again open to the authentic gift of the masculine.

Romance is expressed in rites and rituals

The Church reminds us we are both visible and invisible beings; we express our *interior* selves through *exterior* words, actions, and by use of created things. How else would his beloved know of the poet's love for her unless he spoke it with his lips or penned it with his hands?

We speak with words, but also signs, symbols, and actions.

Romance gives us the language to express love. It's revealed in timeless and even instinctual rites and rituals. The ceremonial signs and words communicate what we feel and what we hold dear, or even sacred, when we:

- clink our champagne glasses at the stroke of midnight,
- toast when a family success is achieved,
- light candles, blow them out, and sing Happy Birthday,
- settle into rocking chairs and sing old lullabies to our babies,
- don robes or tuxedos and sing songs together for special occasions,
- stand, remove hats, and place hands on our hearts to sing the national anthem,
- string lights on trees and wrap presents for others,
- hold coming of age and rites of passage for our teens,

- wear black and veil our faces at funerals,
- chant (or boo!) together at sports events,
- wear uniforms that unite us and identify us to others,
- award trophies and erect statues to honor others,
- throw our hats into the air at graduation,
- line our streets, throw confetti, and salute soldiers in parades,
- ceremoniously cut our cigars, lick the end, and light them up,
- huddle in groups on sports fields,
- or join voices in common songs of celebration, victory, lament, or love.

These are beautiful gestures. Romance embraces and celebrates what is meaningful to us through the beauty of song, dress, music, food, and most especially our bodies. Kisses, hugs, bows, curtsies, handshakes, slaps on the back, and fist-bumps are all expressions of love and connection between people. They are ritualistic and, in that sense, romantic.

Romance is sacramental

Sacramentals are visible objects that open the doors to and provide an intellectual, emotional, or supernatural connection with the Sacred. We have ordinary "sacramentals" in all the things that bring us into the presence of something good: photographs of loved ones, handwritten love letters, a perfumed handkerchief, an old pair of leather gloves. *They do not take the place of the greater object of love; they simply help lead our hearts there.*

A candle may not solve your work-related problems, but it can remind you of the light of God's love and the warmth he brings.

A few fresh flowers won't solve your marriage or money problems, but they can be a comforting reminder of God's beauty and provide a needed consolation.

A hot bath or a cold beer at the end of the day may not get rid of our tough job or nasty client, but it can ease the sorrow and remind us we can rest in God.

Tangible objects are aids. Rites and rituals are doorways. When we allow God to touch our soul or beckon to us through these things, we should see beyond the veil of the created things to the real object of our desire. Hopefully, the time will come in our love for God that we can enjoy but do not need candles, music, or even words to be lifted into his embrace and united in his love.

Reflections

- What did you to do get ready for your first big date?
- What is one of your favorite romantic rituals?
- How do lighted candles change your mood?

Seeing Romance in Religion

*[To St. Francis of Assisi,] his religion was not a
thing like a theory, but a thing like a love affair.*

—G. K. Chesterton[9]

I met up with an old girlfriend who I hadn't
seen since college. We laughed at silly memories while we enjoyed a glass of wine. I began
to tell her about my work as a Catholic author
and speaker.

She smiled and nodded politely, and when I
finished, she matter-of-factly announced, "Well,
I'm definitely spiritual . . . but not religious."

Right. She'd left the Church.

---

[9]   G. K. Chesterton, *Biography of St Francis* (New
York: G.H. Doran Co., 1924).

Our religion is romantic

The word *religion* is commonly believed to come from a Latin word meaning "binding." To the ancients, religion (our relationship with and understanding of God) is what held everything—history, culture, politics, and everything else—together.

Let's face it, though; today religion suffers from a bad reputation. That's because some corrupt people have done really wicked things in the name of religion. But let's not throw out the good with the bad. Instead, let's redeem the truth, and let's lay a foundation first:

- We are both visible and invisible beings.
- We are wooed by an invisible God who became visible.
- When we are finally united with home in heaven, we will be there both body and soul forever.

- Who we are, now and forever, and all our deepest longings are thus expressed both visibly and invisibly.
- True religion unites us—body and soul—with God.

As long as we live, it's impossible to separate our visible from our invisible self. Here's the truth:

- Everyone is "spiritual" because everyone has a spirit.
- Everyone is "religious" because they worship *something*.

If that's true—and it is—then spirituality and religion are not able to be separated.

- Spirituality is our *invisible* set of beliefs, desires, and attachments.
- Religion is how we *visibly* express them in rules, rites, and rituals.

Those who claim to reject religion are fooling themselves. Sure, spirituality detached from outward, structured practices allows one to have sentimental affections, pleasures, and attachment to something good—but on one's own terms and with no responsibility or accountability. That's another distinction people like to make between spirituality and religion: the freedom factor.

In *spirituality*, I submit to no one and I decide what is right and wrong.

In *religion*, I submit to God and the wisdom of his Church.

The truth? We can submit ourselves to God and his Church, retain free will, and still not have to check our brains at the door! But when we don't know or trust him, we must be our own God, or find another palatable substitute. Look at the woman who obsesses about being natural and who communes with a loving cosmic force outdoors instead of with her neighbors at Mass.

Her belief? The body is supreme. "Heaven" is perfect health and beauty.

Her creed? Happiness comes with physical wellness.

Her bible? Best-selling diet and health books.

Her pope? The latest leading diet or exercise guru.

Her pastor? Her personal trainer.

Her patron saints? Athletic stars and unretouched models.

Her rituals? Daily walks, weekly bike rides, eight glasses of water a day.

Her liturgical vestments? Gym shorts and yoga pants.

Her holy communion? Vitamins and supplements.

Her sacred music? Enya.

Her sacramentals? Five-pound weights.

Her mortal sins to be avoided? Pina Coladas and Oreo cookies.

Her confessional? At lunch with girlfriends . . . after a glass of wine.

Whether out of ignorance, naivete, or fear, she has her self-made religion. There is nothing wrong with the gym and supplements. I drink a green spinach smoothie every day and take about ten different vitamins to stay healthy. And I happen to like Enya's music. But true religion is about our relationship with God—not a force of nature.

Most people who resist religion don't understand the beauty of these two oft-maligned characteristics.

Ritualism

The physical, visible structures express our relationship with God. The "smells and bells" of our Church's liturgical traditions would indeed be vain, empty, and idolatrous if they were not appropriately expressing our love for God.

Organization

Organization brings order out of chaos, makes finding things easy, and eliminates unnecessary clutter. Organization is beautiful! But when fear-based rigidity and excessive control sneak in, people run. In any family, and any Church, people will turn away not from "organization" but from a perceived lack of freedom.

Romance has replaced religion

In abandoning religion, even partially, people start to expect romantic relationships to satisfy deep needs that formerly were satisfied through religion: purpose, meaning, belonging, transcendence, unconditional love, wholeness, worth, and communion.

What we got from God, we now want to get—with less strings attached—from our spouse, lover, and friends.

For too many, relationships have become the primary myth of the sacred in our culture. Yikes! What a crushing burden to lay on anyone! You want me to share all your passions and also completely satisfy your deepest existential longings? Sorry . . . I can be romantic, I can give you love, but I can't give you heaven. I can't—and won't—be your God.

Romantic love is a means, not an end

Romance can falsely promise a fast, easy path to transcendence. The initial rush of endorphins released with falling in love and sexual intimacy is an important sign that points to something higher, but we get stuck at the emotional "religious experience." Desire for the ultimate pushes people to pursue the unattainable lover. Secularization has not undone the ache we have for beauty, truth, and goodness (God), but it has redrawn the map.

Romance is often valued over marriage

More and more, the thrill of romance is valued over the long haul of self-sacrificing love in marriage. People want the glorious, heavenly light of the resurrection, but they do not want the cross. They want spirituality, but not religion. We still have the deep needs that God and religion satisfy, but we are looking for a new lover that doesn't make any demands on us. Sadly, such relationships will always collapse under a weight only God and faith can lift and sustain.

Reflections

- What do you do "religiously" every day, and why?
- Have you ever made a romantic relationship the center of your life?
- Do you know anyone who claims to be spiritual but not religious?

Kissing Romance Goodbye

Only the chaste man and the chaste woman are capable of real love.

—Karol Wojtyla (St. John Paul II)[10]

I fell in love for the first time when I was seventeen.

My girlfriend, Gail, and I attended Loretto, the all-girls Catholic high school in Sacramento. We were inseparable—mostly toodling around town in her parents' cute little green VW bug. After school, we'd smoke a cigarette, put on some lip gloss, roll up our skirts at the waist to shorten them, and head over to the all-boys

---

[10]   Karol Wojtyla, *Love and Responsibility* (Boston: Pauline Books and Media, 2013).

Jesuit high school a few miles away. Casually cruising around the parking lot—with the car radio blasting loudly—we'd pretend to look for my brother, Charlie, who we were supposed to be picking up.

One day we struck gold.

Gail and I had gotten out of the car and were chatting with a group of guys and other gals from our school. Suddenly, a car door opened and out stepped Bob, tall and handsome and surfer-boy blonde. I was mesmerized. With his long legs and confident swagger, he slowly headed over to join our group.

"Quick!" said Gail. "Get your year book and you can ask him to sign it."

My heart was pounding as I sucked in my stomach, tossed back my long auburn hair, and smiled.

"Hi," he said.

Oh, God, those eyes.

"Hi," I replied. "Wanna sign my yearbook?"

Bob scrawled something in his fancy, artistic flair that I couldn't even read, but I didn't care. We started talking, and he asked if he'd see me at the party everyone was planning for Friday night.

Squee-e-e! I was in heaven.

"Yes, I think Gail and I will be there . . ."

Bob and I dated all year, mostly at weekend parties with our friends, but every once in a while, he took me out on double-dates and a few alone dates. After the first kiss, I was amazed at how our lips fit so perfectly together (really). A few other girls were visibly jealous and tried to steal him away, but Bob only had eyes for me. We were a couple, and even my little brothers and sisters liked him.

His mom let him drive her sporty red Plymouth Barracuda after school, and sometimes I rode with him to pick her up after her work shift at the hospital. She was always warm, gracious, and very affectionate toward me. Once when I was at their home, she took me to her closet and gave me a lovely blue and green dress that no longer fit her. She thought it would look good on me. It did.

At Christmas, my parents and I went to Bob's house for dinner. While the folks were having cocktails, Bob led me downstairs to his room to serenade me on his guitar with the Beatles' "Norwegian Wood." Five minutes later, my Dad was knocking on the door!

I knew I was too young to get married, but at eighteen, you *do* start to imagine. I loved everything about Bob: his style, the soft pull-over sweaters he wore, his intelligence, artistic talent, sense of humor, how he sang and played the guitar (swoon!), and—yes—that irresistible way he kissed. Even though I hardly knew him, and we rarely talked about anything too deep or important, the thrill of romance was carrying me away.

Romance can hurt

But the dark side was also emerging.

Bob began to pressure me, slowly but consistently, to do things I wasn't ready for. I would push his hands away and everything would be fine for a while. But the next time we went out, he would try again. He started to show his frustration with me, and I felt so rejected and inadequate. Part of me wanted to please him, but I just could not go there. I was so naïve and inexperienced; I never imagined this would be a problem. Wasn't kissing enough?

One night after dinner, Mom let me have the family car to go visit Bob at Baskin Robbins where he worked at the ice cream counter. He looked so handsome in that white uniform with bow tie and little paper hat. I parked, got out of the car, and looked over the dark parking lot into the lit-up storefront. The place was empty except for Bob behind the counter and a tall, sexy blonde leaning toward him—smiling and giggling and flirting like nobody's business. And he was clearly flirting back!

I was *mortified*.

Before he could see me, I ran back to my car and sobbed all the way home. I never said anything to him because I was so insecure and fearful. I went out with him a few times after that, but it had devolved into leaving parties early, getting me alone in the car, and pressuring me.

He finally stopped calling and the relationship ended.

I was crushed.

We can be romanced by sin

The desire to be attached to what is good is good but is ultimately meant for God—the Greatest Good. Other "suitors" (people and things) will compete for our attention, affections, and loyalty. Since God wired us this way, we will all bind and wed ourselves to something or someone because we were made for union. When our vision of goodness is disordered by immaturity, rejection, pride, or fear, we will be tempted to bind ourselves to sin.

With Bob, I knew I might be too young for marriage, but I sure wanted love.

I wanted what Mom and Dad had.

I wanted to be cherished and pursued.

I wanted to belong.

I wanted family.

I wanted everything that romance promised.

Because I felt I could not confide in my parents, lacked wisdom and the language I needed, and was being further seduced by the culture, I soon became easy prey for others who wanted me to "put out" (as we used to say).

I was learning that if I wanted love, I had to give sex.

But, if I gave sex, I was committing sin.

But, if I didn't sin, *I believed I would never have love*.

The choice was easy and, eventually, I was too. Desire and confusion ran through my veins like oil and water. I had not yet learned that chastity is not a rejection of romantic or erotic longings but an ordering of them to the greater good of the persons, in the right time, place, and person. Many years of heartbreak followed.

Romance is often rejected

People will break your heart, and you will break theirs. It's part of life. We need to examine romance with both the idealism of rose-colored glasses and the reality of a microscopic lens. Romance is often rejected for these primary reasons:

It has not been tried because it seems boring

Some people find great delight in and are attached to intellectual, religious, political, or physical pursuits. These, too, are goods that God has given us to be enjoyed properly and in right order. But when people close themselves off to romanticism for these exclusive interests, and surround themselves only with like-minded others, they can become imbalanced. This imbalance hurts them and others.

It has been rejected because of the extremes of others

Giggling, flirting, over-emotional girls—and boys—are a turn off because they are stuck in an extreme. Women who only watch chick-flicks have very little to talk about with others who have broader, more balanced interests. Fussy mothers and/or frivolous fathers will likely produce a few children who want nothing ever to do with any of "that." It's normal when we are turned off by one extreme, that we run to and embrace the other.

It has been tried and found painful

Disappointment, hurt, or abuse in relationship will often shut the door on romantic emotions.

When this happens, normal pessimism no longer balances optimism (as it is meant to do); it replaces it. Romance is no longer sweet; it is cloying. Sentimentality is considered weak, sappy, and maudlin. Starry-eyed lovers are told to come down to earth. Hope flies out the window and passion for life is cooled. Both men and women can be victims of this hardening of the heart. The *last* thing they want to do is read a romantic novel or watch a love story.

Those in this state may pride themselves on having rejected the foolishness of romance—and all its sugar-coated trappings—for a healthy, rational, unvarnished reality. But nothing could be farther from the truth. It seems logical when one is wounded and trying to protect oneself from hurt, but it's irrational to close the door on the other side of reality.

Despite my early heartbreaks, I never gave up on romance. I found out later that the answer is not to reject romance but to redeem it.

Reflections

- What do you remember about the first time your heart was broken?
- Have you ever been "seduced" by the glamour of sin?
- Have you ever felt like romance was a huge disappointment? Why?

PART 2

About Marriage

*You have entered into the most meaning-
ful relationship there is in all human life. It
can be whatever you decide to make it.*[11]

—Ronald Reagan (to his son Michael, 1971)

---

[11] Michael Reagan, *Common Sense of an Uncommon
Man* (Nashville: Thomas Nelson Publishers, 1998).

9

Lusting for Love

*If thou remember'st not the slightest folly
That ever love did make thee run into,
Thou hast not loved.*

—William Shakespeare, *As You Like It*

For some, marriage is a dream

For me, happiness was always going to be the fulfillment of romance: a handsome husband, a cozy home, and lots of kids. I loved being from a large family and wanted to recreate my cheerful childhood. Other girls my age were beginning to pursue careers, but I carried some of my mother's bias, thinking a career was too worldly. But when Prince Charming did not come knocking on my parents' door, I started to panic. I wasn't really aware of it, but my dream was becoming a desperate "lust." Lust isn't always limited to sexual longing; it's present whenever we are highly charged with an intense "gotta have it or I'll just die" attitude. Even when the object we want is good, the desire can be inordinate.

For some, marriage is an escape

After a year of college, I decided to take matters into my own hands. My friends were buying cars and getting apartments. No more curfews for them! I felt trapped and hated being stuck at home. Mom and Dad refused to even think of my going out into the world on my own, and for good reason; for all my education and big-sister responsibility, I was woefully naïve and unprepared for life. My parents were busy supporting and raising all those other kids, and when I announced I was engaged, I think they were both shocked and a bit relieved.

No longer the innocent little school girl, I had met a young man who had just returned from the Vietnam War. He was also lost, emotionally wounded, and struggled with alcohol and pornography. After a few dates, I "suggested" we marry, and he agreed. Yay! I got an apartment, a car of my own, and now I could start having kids. But within just a few months, he went into horrible rages—reflecting his own deeply troubled past of which I had no clue—and he began to take his fists to me.

For some, marriage isn't even marriage

Thank God I had the good sense to call Dad to come get me. In a few short weeks, after unsuccessful attempts at reconciliation, I was in divorce court and in shock. Afterward, Mom advised I would be needing an annulment (what was *that*?), and she filled out all the paperwork for me. The Church called it an "attempted marriage" that lacked the essentials for a true bond. I was numb; I didn't talk with anyone about what had happened or how to move forward. I blamed everything on him. It wasn't until years later—when God began to create a new heart in me—that I realized I had only used this young man to get what I wanted. I didn't love him—I loved romance and the freedom and benefits I thought I would be getting. Since "nothing changes if nothing changes," I quickly found myself in more failed attempts at love.

For some, marriage is an idol

I was on a mission to find a new husband. After the divorce, I went out into the working world, made money, bought a house, a rocking chair, every Dr. Seuss book ever written, and Encyclopedia Britannica for my future kids to do their homework.

I was nesting with a vengeance.

Marriage was less about a lifelong union of a man and a woman than the missing piece of the puzzle for me: you couldn't have your dream of husband-home-kids without a spouse, could you?

In a frenzied haste to satisfy my lust for a family, I then adopted a little eight-year-old girl who no one seemed to want because she was not a newborn and came with particular emotional problems. Now I was a mother! Check.

Next on the list? The husband.

Tragically, I attempted two more short-term marriages, and within a few short years, my adoptive daughter had to leave and go into permanent specialized care. Sadly, my life kept falling apart. I may have looked responsible on the outside, but inside I was lost and out of control. Just like the ancients carved idols out of stone, I had been furiously chipping away at myself and others to create my object of worship: marriage and family.

Telling the truth of my past may sound as if I hardly give it a thought or have somehow minimized it. It was a long time ago; I have been sharing my pitiful story for decades and—trust me—each time a part of me still feels grief and shame.

But God had never taken his divine eyes off me and—like some of us have had to do with our own kids—was waiting for me to hit bottom. When I did, I finally looked up—and scales fell from my eyes.

Shattered romance should wake the slumbering soul

Multiple failed romances finally caused me to finally ask the right questions: How have I gotten myself into this state? Maybe there was something wrong *with me*! Maybe *I* needed to change. I read every self-help book I could find, joined twelve-step groups, and went to more than one therapist.

It was the grace of my baptism that worked its way up through the hard concrete of my ignorance, pride, and sinfulness to reach my heart: *turn to God*, it said.

I prayed to the Lord for help.

I called on Our Blessed Mother for her intercession.

I went to confession for the first time in years.

I started going back to Mass on a regular basis.

I began to listen to Christian radio and the inspiring, life-changing testimonies of men and women on "Focus on the Family's" daily radio broadcasts. Each of them had pursued some "false idol" in a self-directed search for happiness and hit a brick wall. Each of them had finally discovered the love of Jesus Christ for them. They were free.

I wanted what they had.

My last divorce was crushing and humiliating, but this time I knew that I needed to stop the addictive pursuit of happiness on my own terms and stick close to Our Lord. I completed my annulments and began to devour every good book on marriage, relationships, and the devout life I could find. I wanted the truth about what the Church really taught about romance, love, marriage, and sex.

I still had a lo-o-o-ng way to go.

Reflections

- Have you ever failed miserably at marriage in any way?
- What motivated you to keep trying?
- In what area of your life has failure brought change and maturity?

10

Hearing the Bridegroom

At last my love has come along
My lonely days are over, and life is like a song, oh yeah.

—Mack Gordon[12]

R ight before what would eventually become a long, fifteen-plus-year stretch of being single, I had decided to try dating one more time. I thought I was armed with enough truth this time: no sex before marriage and always putting God first.

I met a man at Church (ladies, as some of you may know already, *not* always a guarantee), and we dated chastely for six months. He was smart,

---

[12]   Mack Gordon, "At Last," song from the film *Orchestra Wives*, 1942.

charming, elegant, and even liked to shop! We had spent a delightful day in Beverly Hills and were driving home to the Southern California desert, east along Interstate 10, in the pitch black of night.

"Rose, I'd like to talk about our relationship . . ."

Yes! I was excited. It's always around the six-month mark that dating kicks up a notch toward something more.

"Of course. What's on your mind?"

I was trying to be calm and a bit coy. I wanted to remember this romantic moment and slowly breathed in the heady smell of his cologne and rich scent of the car's leather interior.

"You're so beautiful. You're smart, passionate, and good at what you do. Everyone loves you!"

Oh yeah, this is going to be good. Go on.

"You have such a genuine heart for God and you would make anyone a wonderful wife."

Anyone? What about you?

I started to have an uneasy feeling.

"I really, really like you a lot. Unfortunately, . . . (pause) . . . I think your feelings for me are much more than mine for you."

Argh-h-h-h! No-o-o-o-o.

He was dumping me.

Not again. I felt as if a giant cannonball had just shot through my gut, and I shut my eyes and stopped listening.

Lord, I need you. Come to me now, Please. Let me feel your presence.

Thankfully, I had been practicing the presence of God and learning to run to him instead of other people and things. I suddenly felt the sensation of a strong hand on my right shoulder, and that shocked me.

Then I heard him speak quite clearly to my heart: *Open your eyes and look out the window.*

What?

We were in the middle of nowhere, and I knew there was nothing outside the car but barren Southern California desert and the dark of night. But I had also been trying to hear his voice and obey, even when it did not make sense.

I sighed, opened my eyes, and looked out.

At that very moment, we sped past a billboard with large white block letters on a black background: THE BEST IS YET TO COME.

I closed my eyes again and felt a shiver. I knew

those words were for me from him. I heaved another sigh and realized my date was still yakking away.

Sheesh!

When we got home, I ran inside and threw myself on the bed. Rejected again. Approaching middle age. A failure at love. In shock. I ate some chocolate, said a prayer, and fell asleep.

Repressed desires will beg to be indulged

The next day, I shared my heartbreak with my girlfriend. She said I just needed to try again and that she had lined up a blind date for me for Friday night.

"What?" I cried. "Are you kidding me? Don't you *get* it? I have been divorced *too many times. I am messed up.* I have no business dating. I need to stick with God. Period."

Then, after a few seconds, I asked, "Is he cute?"

Yes, I accepted the date. You can roll your eyes because every time I share this story, I still roll mine. The desire for romance was relentless.

On Thursday, I had driven far from home for

work and briefly stopped at an unfamiliar gro-
cery store for milk. Walking back out to my car,
I heard a male voice behind me.

"Excuse me."

I cautiously turned to see a tall young man
with a beaming smile holding a large bouquet of
fresh-cut flowers he'd obviously just purchased
from the store.

"Here. These are for you."

"Thank you," I said, and briefly looked down
to shift the milk, take the flowers, and open my
purse so I could get the car keys.

A mere second later I looked up and . . . he
was gone.

I whirled myself around on tippy-toes, scan-
ning the entire parking lot. There was no trace
of him anywhere. He had vanished into thin air.

I got into the car and put everything down in
the passenger seat.

Then it hit me.

These are from you, aren't they? I drove off
happy but in shock.

The Gentle Healer will speak to us

On Friday night, I made sure I looked my very best. Catching my reflection in the glass of a framed art print in my living room, I stood and patted my hair into place. The image is of the head of Christ, in profile, entitled "Gentle Healer" by artist Greg Olsen.

Suddenly I saw both the reflection of my face and that of Jesus who seemed to be pressed up into my hair and whispering in my ear.

Rose, Rose, Rose. Don't you know that I am the love you seek?

I froze.

I am the Love that will never leave you or forsake you. I Love You.

At once, a warmth began at the top of my head and shimmered down through my entire body. It was crazy! I was filled with such interior peace and physical lightness that I almost felt weightless.

Something was gone.

At least for that moment, I was free of anxiety, worry, and ego.

I remember going off on the date and for the

first time in my life being present to another person without worrying what he thought of me. He was polite and kind, but he never called me again and I didn't care. I was done.

God had finally reached me through the thing I had most desired: romance.

He had patiently waited.

He had sent me a "love letter" of hope and promise on the billboard.

He has his "angel" deliver me a beautiful bouquet of flowers.

He had spoken "sweet nothings" in my ear in the glass reflection.

God is a patient lover of the soul. To safeguard our free will, he will permit us to choose sin and pain, but he longs for us to return so that he can teach us though them. If we will open our eyes and look out and listen, he will speak to us through our desires.

Reflections

- Have you ever heard God speak directly to your mind and heart?

- Have you ever received a "sign" that you knew was from God?
- Would you like God to woo you more deeply?

Receiving the Gift

*There are in truth three states of the converted:
the beginning, the middle, and the perfection.
In the beginning they experience the charms of
sweetness; in the middle the contests of temptation; and in the end the fullness of perfection.*[13]

—Pope St. Gregory the Great

Shortly after my last date—and swearing off
my mad pursuit of romance—I climbed into
bed one night and began to review the day, but it
turned into a look back at my whole sordid life.

In deep shame and regret, I cried out in my
heart:

---

[13]   Jeffery Richards, *Consul of God: Life and Times of
Gregory the Great* (New York: Routlege and Kegan
Paul, Ltd., 1980).

Lord, all my life I have pursued love, sex, and romance like a freakin' drug addict.

Why?

I only want to love you, but this desire in me for marriage is so powerful.

Why is it there? What does it mean? Can you take it from me? PLEASE.

Almost immediately I heard him again speak interiorly. I'll never forget those words:

Rose, my dear daughter, let your shame instruct you. Let your desires lead you . . . they are a gift!

Haven't you learned that everything in the created world is from me and about me? Everything points up to me. Everything. The deepest desires of your heart also are all about me. Your desires are good, but they have been too limited.

Your desire for marriage points to me and my love for you.

Think about it.

Okay, Lord, I will think about it tomorrow, I promise.

I drifted off to sleep.

About four in the morning, I awoke with seven words running through my mind. From Scripture, I knew that God often spoke to his people in dreams—probably because they were so distracted during the day, he could not get a word in edgewise! Since I knew these seven words were probably important, I fumbled through the dark to find a scratch pad and pencil in the night stand and wrote them down. Then I went back to sleep.

When I woke later that morning, I sat on the edge of my bed and read the words:

> *Invitation*
> *Preparation*
> *Communication*
> *Presentation*
> *Consummation*
> *Generation*
> *Transformation*

It hit me: these are the stages through which romance is meant to progress. Each stage brings it closer to its ultimate fulfillment.

I spent some time thinking about them and came to some startling—but also obvious—truths:

- The first three stages (courtship) *build trust*; the last four (marriage) *forge love*.
- There is a good and right order in these stages. Change the order and you change the outcome.
- Romance between a man and a woman is meant to progress to marriage, and marriage should ultimately transform us—for the good.
- Not all romances are ordered to, or should end up in, marriage. They should end naturally and before sexual intimacy and the partial forging of marital bonds.
- When marital bonds begin to form prematurely, a natural "blindness" sets in. In marriage, this is meant to keep the couple together; in a non-married relationship, it makes the breakup more difficult and much more painful.

I began to see, one more time, that there is a beautiful logic to saving sex for marriage. It blinds you and binds you. In marriage, that is good! Outside marriage, not so much. Let's go a little further into the mystery.

Courtship

Invitation

One party makes it known to the other that they are interested in exploring a relationship. *It is full of promise, but it is not yet a promise.* Hopes and dreams are stirred up and a choice is made: yes, I will see where this may take us, or no, not interested.

Preparation

Once an invitation is accepted, the hope of love rouses them to action! Honestly looking in the mirror, enduring pain, and suffering to be beautiful, they prepare their best for each other. The deepest desire of the heart—and the goal of relationship—is to be seen, understood, and loved for our own sake.

Communication

They begin to communicate more deeply: spoken and unspoken, testing and probing with the questions: *Who are you? Do I like you? What do you want? What can you offer me? Can I trust you? Do you see me? Do you like me? Do you want me? Are you the one?* Some are direct and get right to the point; others sadly never bring up any tough topics. Many only reveal a false self and the other hasn't a clue. This is the stage where it can get stuck, painfully break down, or end.

For many relationships, it *should* end here.

Reflections

- What made you accept or turn down a romantic invitation?
- What is the most memorable thing you've done to prepare for a date?
- What kept you too long in a romantic involvement that should have ended sooner?

12

Following the Recipe

All you need is love.[14]

—John Lennon

The next four stages are distinctly marital.

Ideally, when a relationship is just beginning, the communication stage peaks when there is either a breakup or a marriage proposal. You either buy the dress, or you put it back on the rack. You don't take it home and wear it for six months and then return it. That deprives the rightful shop owner of his due and makes you a user.

Those who opt for sex before marriage and cohabitation are afraid; they want the joys and

---

[14]   John Lennon, "All You Need is Love," July 1967.

pleasures of marriage but with an open back door in the event they want to run. That's why just living together is so harmful because this constant message hums in the background: *I want the pleasures of marriage, but I just don't trust you, or love you enough, to give you my all. And I make no promise to you.*

Let's shorten it:

I don't really love you the way you were made to be loved.

Marriage

Presentation

Presentation is about promises. Making vows gives deeper gravitas to and fundamentally changes any relationship. But only precise promises will result in the creation of a true marriage bond. In a mysterious way, authentic marriage draws the couple into—and unites then with—the mystical marriage of Christ and his Bride. Thus, their vows must bear the same marks of Jesus' promise to the Church.

At the altar, the couple present themselves to each other:

Freely **and without grave pressures,
anxieties, serious reservation, or agendas**

Nobody wants to marry another who is wrongly motivated, being forced, is too scared, or too selfish to love freely and completely. The relationship will suffer and ultimately break down. Love demands this type of freedom. Otherwise it is not really love.

Fully, **with nothing held back and nothing hidden**

Would you feel loved if someone has left the back door open for escape or divorce when things get tough? Would it be true love if the person withheld some important truth or asset from you? Love demands total willing surrender of all that one is and has. Otherwise it is not really love.

Faithfully, **with no other passion or
relationship in higher order in the heart**

Would you feel loved and safe if your spouse has the option to intimately or sexually bond with another? Would it give you peace to know that—if it came to a choice—he would pick his mother, father, work, or money over you? Love demands fidelity to your greatest good. Otherwise it is not love.

Fruitfully, with an openness to and respect for the gift of fertility of the other

People don't want the inconvenience of children, but husband and wife are ordered in every way to become fathers and mothers—even when there's a physical impossibility such as illness, old age, or infertile periods. To close oneself off selfishly or improperly to the fruit of love is not love.

This is the kind of love for which we were made—and for which we all long. These vows make the marriage come into being right then and there! That's why most ministers say, "I now present Mr. and Mrs. You may kiss the bride!"

Sadly, if these specific promises are missing or defective (i.e., one cannot live up to them), then the relationship can be many things, but not really a true marriage.

Consummation

Con means "together," and *summa* means "the very highest." Once the couple promises the highest form of human relationship *in words*, they then express wedding vows *in body language*. They remain two separate people but mysteriously also become "one flesh." When a couple physically expresses wedding vows, they strengthen the one-flesh bond.

Generation

Male and female bodies are designed so that in the marital act the man can make the woman a mother; her body functions to make him a father. Hormones bond them to each other emotionally and to facilitate the possibility of new human life. This is meant to create and ensure the safest, healthiest, and most loving environment in which the couple can thrive, and a child can grow. Sex is meant for both bonding and babies. Our bodies as male and female make no sense without the other!

Transformation

These lifelong promises and intimate encounters change us. In the day-to-day, year-to-year commitment, we should be transformed from self-focused individuals to a union of souls. Our rough edges are smoothed, our fears lessened, our trust increased, and our hearts enlarged. It takes time, work, patience, and the ability to ride waves of disappointment and pain.

But it is worth it!

Many people even remark that old married couples often end up finishing each other's thoughts and even looking like each other. In such a beautiful and total merging of souls, the individuals are not diminished or lost. They retain all of their unique and unrepeatable selves, but they grow to be their best.

The seven stages are the recipe for romance

Have you ever ruined a recipe? It's easy to understand that the wrong ingredients, cheap substitutes (margarine!), or ignoring the directions will end up in a disaster—or at least something edible but unrecognizable. It's the same with

love: what should look and "taste" like a beautiful romance can often be something else entirely.

Some of the ways we ruin the seven-stage recipe for romance include:

We skip important stages

Too often we avoid getting to know the whole
person. For some, it's too much work or responsibility. In that, we reject their goodness. When
someone rarely asks you about yourself, or cares
about your interests, the unspoken message is
"You are not worth it."

For others, we avoid full self-disclosure or getting to know them fully out of fear of discovery.
Some people so desperately want to be coupled
or married—and desire the pleasures or perceived security of the next stages of romance—
that they don't want any reality to jeopardize the
dream or get in the way of the agenda. Worms?
What worms?

We rush into stages

With an increasingly sexualized culture, even
sincere Catholic men and women can end up

being sexually intimate on the first "date." When that happens, we are no longer connoisseurs of gourmet love, we are emotionally hungry dogs; we jump right into consummation, grasping greedily at the emotional and physical pleasures that come with sex. When we are done chewing on that bone, we drop it and totter off—saliva still dropping from our jowls—in search of the next tasty treat. Too many also feel that they are the ones who have been emotionally gnawed clean and then spit out on the floor.

We avoid the necessary hard work

Imagine spending hours in the kitchen preparing a fine dish and then never sticking it into the oven. That's what happens in some relationships when some people avoid the heat that comes with a tried and true romance. They aren't hungry enough for the finished product and have, instead, learned to just enjoy scraping the bowl and "licking their fingers." Yes, they have avoided the 400-degree demands of love, but in their laziness, they have also deprived themselves of the delicacies and true satisfaction of love.

Laziness in love is never loving

Reading instruction in our elementary schools used to include highly moralistic and religious texts to teach literacy. We were learning to read and how to love and be virtuous at the same time. I remember the old English folktale of *The Little Red Hen* about the importance of hard work and the shame, as well as the consequences, of laziness.

In the fable, the little red hen finds a grain of wheat and excitedly asks for help from the other farmyard animals to plant it, but they all refuse.

At each later stage (harvest, threshing, milling the wheat into flour, and baking the flour into bread), the hen again asks for help from the other animals, but again she doesn't receive any help.

Finally, the hen sets the fresh-baked bread on the window sill where the fragrant aroma fills the barnyard and draws all the animals. Everyone wants a piece! But she tells them that since no one worked for the result, they will not get to participate in the rewards.

Romance is like that grain of wheat. It must

be planted and given the time to grow into love. The truth must be harvested, the ego crushed, and the purifying fires of self-sacrifice turn it into food that truly feeds the soul. Laziness is not love. Like anything else, romance that results in the greatest good requires work (see Prv 10:4).

Reflections

- Where do you think most people stay stuck in these seven stages and why?
- Why do you think that sexual intimacy creates a deep bond that is hard to break?
- If you are, or have been, married, how has it changed you? Why?

13

Searching the Scriptures

When the Christian prays, he is seeking nuptial union with the Lord.[15]

—Joseph Cardinal Ratzinger

As I continued to ponder the seven stages, I thought back to my First Holy Communion. It was such an exciting day, and our class had prepared for it for almost a year. At seven years old, I was beyond thrilled to dress like a little bride and wear the lace veil and organza dress with delicate sheer tulle overlay. I am still moved by the beautiful song we sang and will never forget the words:

---

[15]   Joseph Cardinal Ratzinger, *Spirit of the Liturgy* (San Francisco: Ignatius Press, 2000).

Oh Lord I am not worthy
That Thou shouldst come to me
But speak Thy words of comfort
And healed my soul shall be.

And humbly I'll receive Thee
THE BRIDEGROOM OF MY
SOUL
No more by sin to grieve Thee,
Nor fly Thy sweet control.

—Author and composer unknown

Bridegroom? I finally got it! Romance was a picture of God's love for mankind—for me. Could it be that what I had learned and experienced about romantic relationships—good and bad—would help me better understand yet another aspect of my relationship with the Lord?

Our bodies have a theology

I was so excited.

I met with Father Kidder who, as you may remember from my book on happiness, was the Catholic camp director who caught me and my friend, Gail, using his razor to shave our legs when we were teenagers. Despite that and other little adolescent mishaps, we had remained good friends for many years, and I was eager to share with him my seven stages of romance.

"This sounds a lot like *Theology of the Body*," he told me.

"What's that?" I asked.

"Pope John Paul II wrote it. It's a collection of his weekly addresses from 1979 through 1984. It's a beautiful Bible study, really, about what it means to be human, to be male and female. It's all about human love in the divine plan. Here, take this and read it."

He plopped a large and heavy volume in my hands.

Gulp. The print was small, and the words were big.

I spent weeks getting through it all, but it was rich and dense. It is a spectacular vision of the beauty, dignity, and true purpose of being male and female. And it answered all the deep and troubling questions I had. *It gave flesh to the seven stages of romance God had given me.*

Marriage was and is God's idea

Did you know your feminine body reveals the ultimate meaning of life itself?

Stamped right into our bodies as male and female is the call to come together in a love that is life-giving. Men are made for women; women are made for men. When they unite physically—and in a way that is truly loving and rightly ordered—they become a pale, imperfect, but beautiful image of God pursuing and possessing each soul in a perfect union of hearts. Our bodies are not just biological—they are theological!

Whoa! Do you see it? In a sense, God wants to "marry" us.

John Paul II fell in love with human love and made it the central theme of his priesthood, preaching, and writing. He knew there was great dignity and transcendence in the call of man and woman to become one. And the key to understanding love and living it out rightly? To infuse the *passion* of human romantic love with the *purity* of divine, self-sacrificing love. Eros and agape—two sides of the same coin never meant to be separated.

The Polish pontiff eloquently draws out and addresses Scripture's "spousal analogy" where God wanted to "wed" his people and Jesus come to us as or Bridegroom. I realized that:

- the love of husband and wife points to the love of God for man,
- the heart's desire for romance is the desire for union with God,
- earthy marriage points to the heavenly marriage,
- and the natural order of love, marriage, and sex illuminates the spiritual order.

The Bible begins and ends with romance and marriage

This romantic imagery has been around for thousands of years. It was like a pair of glasses that suddenly corrected my narrow and clouded vision and helped me see the beautiful truth:

- The Bible begins with the marriage of Adam and Eve.

- God reveals his love for his people as a husband to his bride.
- The Song of Solomon is erotic love poetry that reveals God's desire for us.
- Jesus reveals himself as the Bridegroom, come to rescue and wed his Bride.
- Heaven is the eternal wedding feast of Jesus and the Bride (the Church).

Most religions talk about honoring, obeying, or seeking after God, but Christianity turns it around to God's first seeking after *us*! The prophet Isaiah, in a shocking and magnificent message, says to the people Israel, "Your builder (God) wants to marry you" (see Is 62:5). God wants us to be intimately one with him—starting now but lasting through all eternity!

I think back to a time in my childhood in our kitchen just before dinner. Mom and Dad were lip-locked in a tight embrace, and I loved seeing their bodies melt together. Nothing but pure, tender mama-and-daddy love and goodness shone out of that scene, and without even thinking, I remember jumping up out of my chair and running into their embrace. They laughed as I squeezed myself in between them and let myself be smooshed by their bodies. Caught up in their embrace, it was as if their love passed through and flowed into me too. I never wanted to leave that warm, safe place. What a gloriously beautiful image of where I came from—their physical union—and where I wanted to stay. It's an icon that points all of us to the divine embrace of love from which we came, and where we are meant to remain forever.

Reflecting on this later helped me to realize:

God is not just a benevolent deity here to grant our heart's desires.

Our desires—for people, places, things—point beyond themselves to him, the fullest blessing, the greatest love, the most perfect union of hearts, minds, bodies, and souls: the mystical marriage of every soul with God.

Marriage is a sign and a doorway to heaven.

As Catholics, we know marriage isn't merely a visible sign, but through its sacramental nature, it's also a portal of sorts; a sign and a doorway at the same time. Entering into it in the right way can transport us into another realm and unite us in some mysterious way with that eternal embrace of Christ and his Bride.

Spouses can access divine powers (grace)!

Imagine! Caught up in that mystical union, spouses (aware of it or not) can draw on the powerful supernatural graces that flow between Jesus and the Church in that divine spousal embrace. Grace helps us love each other.

What a stunning vision for human sexuality! The "theology of the body" reveals our invitation into a mystical marriage that is stamped right in our bodies as male and female. Sex is far greater than just us, and it points to something supremely sublime.

This, at last, was the answer to the deepest ache of my heart.

With God's grace—and this new insight—I stopped frantically pursuing romance with others. As I opened up to the wisdom of the Church, God opened doors for me to be able to help others pick themselves up from broken relationships.

And for the next couple of decades, God made his claim on my heart, showed me more of his love, and helped me make him my First Love.

Reflections

- Does the image of Jesus as a loving Bridegroom appeal to you or not? Why?
- Did your parents show physical affection in front of you? If so, how did you feel?
- Does the idea of earthly marriage as a sign of God's love for you make sense?

14

Wooing the Soul

Christianity is God's marriage proposal to the soul.[16]

—Peter Kreeft

No wonder I had always been drawn to romance—my world was a wedding all along, and I never knew it. I stepped through the romance portal and began to reflect on the seven stages in my own life and saw I had been stuck "dating" God and had never surrendered fully to him. I'd learned to let him court me, but he wanted more—he wanted marriage. So I prayed intently and finally said yes.

---

[16] Peter Kreeft, *Yes or No: Straight Answers to Tough Questions About Christianity* (San Francisco: Ignatius Press, 1991).

Invitation

"Fear not, for I have redeemed you. I have called you by name, you are mine" (Is 43:1).

At baptism, my parents had arranged my "marriage" with God, accepting the Bridegroom's proposal on my behalf. As the *Catechism* observes, "The entire Christian life bears the mark of the spousal love of Christ and the Church."[17] In the "mystical marriage," he still beckons me deeper into the interior. Some days I pack up my bags and can't wait to go; at other times, I still resist. Because he wants our yes to be freely given, he will always *propose*, never *impose*. And even after we have given him our heart, he continually invites us more deeply into his love.

Preparation

"Create in me a clean heart, O God, and put a new and right spirit within me" (Ps 51:10).

In second grade, the nuns prepared us to receive Jesus in a special way in our first Holy Communion. Jesus wanted to live in our hearts,

---

[17]   CCC 1617.

they said, but only if we would invite him in. I remember the illustrations in our catechism that had a little door on the heart. That door, I realize now, signified the freedom we have to let him in or—God forbid—keep him out. But no one wants to come into a heart that stinks of sin and selfishness. God himself would help clean up our souls when we went to him on confession. So, in the sacrament of Penance, he purified us, and in Confirmation, he makes a beautiful place for himself to dwell.

Communication

"I call upon you, for you will answer me, O God; incline your ear to me, hear my words" (Ps 17:6).

God communicates himself to us in everything: nature, music, art, food, through others, in Scripture, and through his Church. Prayer and obedience are the way we communicate with God. Our prayers can be mental, written, spoken, spontaneous, formal, individual, communal, or sung. They can be our acts of love and service and even the daily work we do. Anything offered to and for God is an expression, a communication, of our love for him. Any cry of the heart is communication.

Now, these movements of the mind and heart are good, but they are only the beginning of the divine romance—but not its desired end. God wants all of us.

He wants marriage, not just courtship.

Presentation

"Mary took a pound of costly ointment of pure nard and anointed the feet of Jesus and wiped his feet with her hair; and the house was filled with the fragrance of the ointment" (Jn 12:3).

We were made for consummation; it is a frustrating and even maddening place to stay stuck in courtship. The time must come when we offer God all we have—nothing held back.

Mary's humble presentation of herself and her gift to Jesus was not one of fearful servitude but joyful gratitude. When we present ourselves to Christ, whether it be the first time as an adult or thereafter throughout our days, we do so always recalling our littleness and his tender mercies and abundant love. When we know how loved we are, and remember how he gave himself completely for us, we don't even have to think about what our response might be; his grace expands our hearts and overcomes our concupiscence so we can offer him *our* very best.

Consummation

"For this reason, a man shall leave his father and mother and be joined to his wife" (Mk 10:7).

God wants sweet and complete union with us. Jesus left his heavenly home to pursue us, his beloved. He left his Father and mother and went to the cross to consummate his love for us. We don't need to abandon our other loves—family, spouse, and even our own children—but we do need to place them in their proper order in our hearts. With God's grace, we must come to a place where he alone has our "first fruits" of love. Nothing else in the way. Nothing blocking his graces and life-giving love. From our own sweet surrender to his love, he lifts us up and pulls us into his embrace.

Generation

"I came that they may have life, and have it abundantly" (Jn 10:10).

God has revealed himself with masculine imagery for a reason; just as a husband enters a woman from without to impregnate her, so God creates the world from without rather than birthing it from within himself. He invites us as "other" to join him, where he initiates out of love. Just as a woman cannot impregnate herself, so the universe cannot create itself. Nor can the soul fill itself with divine life.

When we allow God to tenderly lift and totally possess us, powerful graces burst forth from him and implant themselves within the "womb" of our heart and begin to grow into the virtues.

We will deliver that love to others, usually not without the occasional bouts of "morning sickness" that come as we begin detaching from prior selfish ways of life. It's painful to let go of old, comfortable habits and ways of thinking. Big changes like this can sometimes leave us feeling emotionally queasy in the beginning.

We definitely will have certain "cravings" for

that which will support the new life growing within us. I remember being surprised at wanting to watch more Catholic television programs, hungering for more prayer time, and becoming bored with trivial things. We will also have "stretchmarks" as his love expands our hearts to fuller and fuller capacity! As Jesus bore the evidence of his love for us in the scars of his hands and feet, our hearts will bear these maternal wounds of love too.

Sometimes, when our lives begin to change after intimate encounters with him and we recall or long for the old ways, we may fall into forms of "postpartum depression." Sometimes our former desires will refuse to let us go; a good spiritual director can help with these big changes in our lives.

And, with this analogy, a thought that often delights me is that just as our natural children look like both their parents, the good works that are conceived in us will also image both of us. His "features" are all that is good, true, and beautiful in our acts, but our own preferences, temperaments, and talents will also color and shape the good we do. Sandra's time volunteering in a mission will look a bit different than Beth's time giving up her favorite television time for her aged father, or Elizabeth's time teaching catechism. But all three women will "give birth" to these acts of love by first being filled with love by the same God.

Transformation

"Therefore, let us leave the elementary doctrines of Christ and go on to maturity" (Heb 6:1).

In the spiritual life, just as in earthly marriage, true love is not found in the bursts of passionate emotions but in the long-term commitment and the day-to-day interactions of admiration, respect, kindness, devotion, love, struggle, fidelity, and even the tears and joyful laughter. Friendship.

It only takes a few minutes for a bride and groom to wed, but a lifetime of two wills clashing, kissing, and making up for them to build a solid marriage. When we receive Christ, an initial moment of commitment will continue into a lifetime of adjusting—running, returning, kissing, and making up. The earthly reality reveals the spiritual reality! The popular saying is that "God loves you just as you are, but he also loves you enough that he doesn't want you to stay that way!"

With God, we never lose our uniqueness, but we will begin to mirror him. Like an old married couple who finishes each other's sentences, we will even start to think with "the mind of Christ" (see 1 Cor 2:16)!

God wants our daily abandonment to his love

Holiness—and ultimately our highest happiness—is entering and being lifted up into God's love day after day. Abandonment is not a bad word, but when we don't trust, it sounds devastating. Immediately it evokes images of having nothing, being alone, and starving to death. That's how it feels when we are abandoned.

But "abandonment to God" is actually rejecting emptiness and choosing abundance! If you were sitting in a dingy church basement eating that same old ham sandwich, apple, and chocolate chip cookie that usually get served at parish events, and Father said, "Hey everyone, come to the rectory! We have filet mignon, fresh shucked oysters on the half-shell, homemade gnocchi with brown-butter sage sauce, and top-shelf cocktails!"

You can bet I would hurriedly "abandon" the folding steel chair and the boxed lunch for something far better. That's what "abandonment to God" is all about.

Reflections

- Does the thought of total abandonment to God make you uneasy? Why?
- What area of your life does he still want you to give him?
- What pleasures and attachments are hardest for you to release and why?

15

Appraising the Analogy

*The truth does not change according to our
ability to stomach it emotionally.*[18]

—Flannery O'Connor

This daring, nuptial picture of the relationship between God and the soul has both
merit and limits; some people are not able to
think clearly about sexual differences, love, and
procreation, especially as a living sign of something greater.

They can be shocked and offended at any
attempt to relate married love—most particularly

---

[18]   Flannery O'Connor, "6 September (1955): Flannery O'Connor to Betty Hester," *The American
Reader*, http://theamericanreader.com/6-septem-
ber-1955-flannery-oconnor/.

the raw, sexual dimension—to God. It's true; we would be foolish to attempt to bring God down to our level. Sadly, some have erred that way, in a profane stance rooted in ignorance or pride. But, remember, it is God himself who gave us this mysterious and passionate imagery. Instead of dragging the divine down, it is meant to be a doorway that leads us upward. Even when it confuses or turns us off, it is still true.

The spousal analogy has value and limits

Whether we see it as sign, symbol, or metaphor, it will eventually collapse under the weight of both our limitation and frailties and God's unimaginable transcendence. Still the spousal mystery has great value because God gave it to us, the Church affirms it, and, well . . . it just makes sense.

Our vocabulary has to be purified and tested by the whole of Scripture and tradition. Because our culture has separated *eros* from *agape*, the erotic part of romance has become tainted with self-centered pleasure seeking. That which should be the icon, leading us to a greater understanding of God's love, becomes the idol.

To keep from improperly regarding the gift of the spousal imagery, let's remember:

Every woman is made for and is looking for Jesus

So is every man. The problem is that when we don't draw near to or have authentic relationship with Christ, we will inappropriately seek his substitutes in others. We can make idols out of men. We can make idols out of romance, and marriage, and even our children.

Looking for Jesus, we can be drawn to priests

Some understandably make false gods out of their priests. Acting in a special way in the person of Christ, priests' lips speak words of consecration that call down the divine power of the Holy Spirt. Their hands confect the Eucharist—the Body, Blood, Soul, and Divinity of Jesus made present to us. They can forgive sins. They can bless and curse. Without them, we have no Mass. Even if they struggle with sin, their priesthood is worthy of awe, respect, and love. In some sense, they are the closest living representative of Jesus on earth. Yes, we should all be attracted to them and love them. But those who have romantic feelings for, or improperly fall in love with, a priest are still longing for and seeking Christ. Despite this understanding, the desire is still misplaced and maybe even idolatrous, and will only bring frustration, pain, and even temptation to sin. If you find yourself in this situation, get to confession, take whatever steps are necessary to avoid temptation, and ask God for the grace to re-order your deep longings to him and him alone.

Jesus is not your boyfriend

We should never reduce God to a spiritual boyfriend. Lonely single women or those in unhappy marriages can find men disappointing when compared to the perfect and handsome ideal of Bridegroom Jesus. Especially when in our minds he looks like *The Passion of the Christ*'s Jim Caviezel!

Semi-erotic and romantic language is not mean to pull God down into our emotional or sexual bedrooms. The divine won't fit into our limited understanding and experience. Instead, we need to lift what we understand about romance up to its highest dimensions where it leads us to the mystical marriage. If we stay stuck in a low level of understanding, we will miss the real Bridegroom.

Saints and mystics embraced this imagery

There are some seventy or more historical saints—men and women—who have reported or were known to have experienced this mystical marriage in a profound way. Some of them include:

St. Augustine (354–430) wrote of the mystical marriage; he saw the blood and water flowing from Jesus's side as his "spiritual seed" that gives life to the world. He said, "Like a bridegroom Christ went forth from his chamber. . . . He came to the marriage-bed of the cross, and there in mounting it, he consummated his marriage. And when he perceived the sighs of the creature, he lovingly gave himself up to the torment in place of his bride and joined himself to [her] forever" (*Sermo Suppositus* 120).

St. Mechtilde (1241–1298), a German mystic who wrote that Christ's "noble nuptial bed was the very hard wood of the Cross on which he leaped with more joy and ardor than a delighted bridegroom" (cited by Blaise Arminjon in *The Cantata of Love*).

St. Catherine of Siena (1347–1380), who received a diamond and pearl wedding ring from Jesus; in a moment of ecstasy and intense pain, Jesus opened her side and placed his heart within her bosom.[19] Some testified to have witnessed the scar.[20]

St. John of the Cross (1542–1591) is renowned for his pure and passionate poetry on what happens when the soul opens like a bride to the Beloved. "Just as in the consummation of carnal marriage there are two in one flesh . . . so also when the spiritual marriage between God and

---

[19]   Pope Benedict XVI, "Catherine's Heart," EWTN, http://www.ewtn.com/library/papaldoc/b16Chrst-Chrch130.htm.

[20]   Jeanne Marie, "Saint Catherine of Siena," Catholicism.org, June 14, 2008, https://catholicism.org/saint-catherine-of-siena.html.

the soul is consummated, there are two natures in one spirit and love" (Commentary on stanza 22:3 of the *Spiritual Canticle*).

St. Teresa of Avila (1515–1582) is the feisty and passionate Carmelite sister known for her complete surrender to God and her spousal prayer forms, including physical and spiritual ecstasies.[21]

St. Elizabeth of the Trinity (1880–1906), a French religious and mystic often talked about how being a bride of Christ is to have an exchange of hearts . . . and to have all rights to his heart![22]

As a wife should share in the life of her husband, and as Christ suffered for the redemption of mankind, the mystical spouse enters into a more intimate participation in his sufferings. The "mystical marriage" comes with the stigmata, martyrdom, and heavy trials. Union with Jesus is ultimately union with him on the cross.

The forerunner of intimate union with Christ is purification of the soul by interior and exterior

---

[21]   Teresa of Avila, *The Autobiography of St. Teresa of Avila* (Rockford: TAN Books, 1997).
[22]   Elizabeth of the Trinity, *The Complete Works of Elizabeth of the Trinity*, vol. 1 (Washington, DC: ICS Publications, 1984).

trials. And this is the beauty of Church teachings on purgatory: it is suffering that will burn away the last remaining attachments to free the soul for union with God.

As St. Rose of Lima reportedly said, "The only ladder whereby we get to heaven is the cross."

You are already a saint in the making

Don't be discouraged after reading about the saints. They all started where you and I did: with an inordinate love for self, a fear of losing comfort and pleasure, and many began with a rather pathetic and weak love for God. Their eventual moments of ecstasy or rapture were surprising to them and not ongoing. But God is still in the business of sanctifying and making us beautiful when we give him our hand and say, "Yes!"

Your path to union with him will be unique and unrepeatable. Don't worry too much about signs or stigmata. You will have everyday suffering in measures that you can bear with his grace, and it is precisely those that will serve as your personal doorway to heaven. Just ask him to stretch open your heart and fill it with love and divine graces; sincerely ask for an increase in your desire for him, and the rest will follow.

Remember:

God loves your ordinariness.
God will redeem your desires.
God longs for all of your heart.
God will always love you where you are.

The Seven Stages are cyclical

In the lesser sense, you can move through all seven stages in a minute. From an awareness of hearing his invitation to be with him, you can prepare, stop what you're doing, or focus on him. Then you can communicate your "yes" and present yourself to him, to be taken up in prayer and love, filled with his love and life, and transformed.

In a deeper sense, your relationship with him can—and should—reach all seven stages before the end of your life. Your advancement—by his grace—will move you into the mystical marriage in real but imperfect consummation and transformation as the saints have discovered.

In the most complete sense, however, life on earth can only move through the first three stages. We will only fully present ourselves and be taken up into the eternal embrace and changed forever when we reach heaven.

The Bridegroom image of God is a unique and primary analogy, but not the only one. We can—and should—also relate to him as a loving father, a caring shepherd, a fair master, and a potter who lovingly shapes us into his masterpieces. I hope you will embrace and delight in these meditations on God as Husband to his people and Bridegroom to the Church. They are rich and romantic!

But God is bigger and more mysterious than any analogy we have—even the ones he has given us himself.

Reflections

- What makes you most uneasy about the "spousal analogy," and why?
- What do you think Jesus looks like? Do you have a favorite artistic image of Christ that deeply appeals to your heart?
- Where are you now, and where would you like to be, in the spiritual life?

16

Accepting the Proposal

*When you realize you want to spend the rest
of your life with somebody, you want the rest
of your life to start as soon as possible!*[23]

—Harry (*When Harry Met Sally*)

Invitation

In 2009, I received a notice that my forty-year
high school reunion was being held in Sacramento, CA. The two all-girls schools and the
two all-boys schools (Jesuit and Christian Brothers) would have a joint celebration at the Dante
Club. I was thrilled!

---

[23]   Nora Ephron, *When Harry Met Sally*, 1989.

I marked the date on my calendar and immediately thought of Bob. I hadn't seen him since the early seventies but heard he'd married and divorced. Was he still single? Was he still handsome? Was he still a jerk?

I called the reunion committee chairman.

"Hey, John, it's Rose Sweet. How *are* you?"

"Hey, Rosie! Blah-blah-blah . . ."

"Blah, blah, blah . . . hey, um, by the way . . . is Bob Makohin registered?"

In my fifties and still trying to act cool.

"Yeah, he is! And, funny, he asked about you!"

Gulp.

I'd been single for decades and was doing just fine. I must admit, though, the prospect of romance with my old high school flame was still exciting. I imagined by now he had grown up and learned how to love a woman the right way. There was so much I didn't know, but I was willing to find out.

Over the next few months, I didn't think much about the reunion until a few weeks before. It was an eight-hour drive up north from Southern California where I lived, and I planned to stay a week and also visit old friends. But on Monday, my associate walked out with no notice and left me with several large unfinished projects and looming deadlines. The reunion was Saturday.

There was no way I could go now.

I was shocked, hurt, and angry. I felt sorry for myself but decided to get over it and move on. In my life, love had come and gone again too many times. I worked like crazy all week, and by Friday afternoon, I was surprised to be about 90 percent caught up.

Hm-m-m. Could I go? If I got up early and drove all day, I could get there on time and then come back the next morning and be back for work on Monday. I ran home, picked out a cute outfit, and went to bed early. I drove all day, pushing the maximum speed limit, freshened up at a girlfriend's, got to the reunion, and walked up to the bar.

There he was.

Handsome as ever.

My stomach flip-flopped and that surprised me. He was looking and smiling at me, which gave me the courage to smile back.

"Hey, Bob Makohin!"

"Hey, Rosie Sweet!"

All he needed from me was the okay to proceed, and he did.

The rest of that night we hit it off like old times and enjoyed each other, our old friends, and we all danced to the music of the sixties.

I felt like Cinderella leaving the ball when he asked me to join a group going out for coffee afterwards.

"No, sorry, I have to get some sleep for my five-hundred-mile drive home in the morning. But why don't you come see me sometime?"

I gave him my business card since I didn't have a glass slipper.

Preparation

A few weeks and a couple of phone calls later, Bob drove eight hours from the San Francisco Bay area to the Southern California desert to see me. He washed and gassed up his car and I spent days making myself as pretty as possible. Now that I understand what was happening, we were preparing to be gifts to one another—hoping to be appreciated and received with delight.

And I was rehearsing exactly what I wanted and needed to say.

Communication

Part of my past problems was that I did not understand the truth of who I was nor did I have the language to express my deepest desires. I had also been afraid of pushing potential love away and was willing to settle for something less than I really wanted or needed.

This time I knew I did not need a relationship to be happy or fulfilled.

I knew I would never settle for less than the vision Christ had given us.

If any man wanted to court me, he had to share the same vision.

Like many of my girlfriends, I'd read countless relationship books that touted all "the rules" for attracting and keeping Mr. Right. Most of those techniques were wrong, especially the one that advised not revealing too much about yourself too soon: play it cool, string him along. I agreed in theory with that when it came to other things, but not the essentials. Out of love, fairness, and honesty, I had to let Bob know exactly where I stood on the very first date. Why waste his time or mine? I refused to drag things out to get three or four more expensive dinner dates.

I'll never forget how excited I was when Bob drove into my driveway. We went to dinner, got past the usual pleasantries, and then—as relationship experts would say—I broke all the rules: I poured out my heart and launched into one of my best sixty-second presentations of "Theology of the Body."

"Bob, I need to share something right away with you."

"Okay," he said. "Sure."

Gulp.

"Well . . . *I need to let you know that I have made a lot of mistakes in my life, and for the first time, I know exactly who I am and why I am here and where I am going.*

I know what it means to be Catholic, and I am deeply and faithfully devoted to God. I don't want to just date anyone to simply have a good time.

If you are not open to the possibility of marriage and are not looking for a faithful spouse, then we need to end it right here and now.

I don't want to play games with anyone, and I refuse to use you.

I will not have sex before marriage—so don't expect it—not because it's some antiquated Church rule but because I now understand the dignity of the human person and the beautiful and powerful meaning of sex. I know what it does and how we violate each other when we put the cart before the horse.

I want to love you and every other person in the way God intended and to do things right and go higher, and I never, ever want to displease God again. If you can accept that, fine. If not, then have a nice life."

I stopped, shocked at my own boldness, and needing a deep breath.

Would he listen to me? Would he hear me? Is he going to ridicule me? Is he going to go away?

Bob was struck dumb for a second and then quipped, "Whew! And here I was thinking we were going to have a few drinks!"

I laughed . . . mostly out of relief that he used a bit of humor to lighten the mood.

It was a lot to dump on someone, I know. But I was still determined. I climbed down off my soapbox, took a sip of my wine, and continued in a thoughtful manner.

"Bob . . . be honest. Aren't you tired of being used by women?"

His eyebrows rose slightly. I didn't know much about him or his past, but I know our generation and I know the human heart. He'd shared that he'd had his fill of unsuccessful relationships and really hated the whole middle-aged dating thing.

He reflected quietly then said, "Yeah, I am."

I leaned in for the kill.

"And . . . aren't *you* tired of using women?"

He was shocked, but a few seconds later, he replied by quietly nodding his head.

I didn't know what else to say, so I shut up and let myself be present to Bob and to the moment.

"Rose, you're right. I *am* tired of dead-end relationships. But, look at us. What's the answer? Is there any other way?"

"Yes! There *is* a different way, Bob. For the first time in my life, I know what it is. Won't you consider being open to exploring it?"

Bob didn't run away that night, and we continued to talk, pushing past the surface and getting down to what really mattered.

Romance seeks the truth

I was sad to hear of Bob's previous attempt at marriage years earlier and a painful divorce. It was a union that produced three fine sons but a lot of heartache for a long time. To be transparent, and to come to a deeper understanding of our strengths and weaknesses, we eventually shared our annulment details with each other. We were subconsciously asking the questions: *Do I like you? Do you like me? Can I trust you? Are you the one?*

When I was satisfied that Bob was indeed looking for and available for marriage the way God intended, we attended a week-long "Head and Heart: Theology of the Body" retreat with Christopher West in Amish country Pennsylvania. Regardless of any future we might have or not, together we would more deeply explore God's vision for marriage.

We were both scared and excited at the same time. We had long talks, ups and downs, a few arguments, and lots of laughs together. We took turns visiting each other when we could. Bob eventually introduced me to his sons—each of whom immediately stole my heart—and then later drove down to the Southern California desert again and proposed.

My heard was spinning and my heart was bursting.

Reflections

- If you're married, what did you love most about your spouse's proposal?
- If you're still single and hoping, what would he say to sweep you off your feet?
- What would you do if the man you loved never proposed?

17

Feasting at the Banquet

The LORD *of Hosts will make for all peoples a feast
of fat things, a feast of choice wines—of fat things
full of marrow, of choice wines well refined.*

—Isaiah 25:6

Presentation

Neither of us wanted a huge ceremony.
Despite our age, we were both still open
to whatever God wanted to reveal to us, so we
attended a marriage preparation class and met a
few times with his pastor, Father Healy. The day
before our small wedding, Bob, my three new
stepsons, and I all went to confession.

We married on the feast of St. John the

Baptist, and only a handful of close family and friends were there when we presented ourselves to each other with all the same hopes and fears every couple has. We made vows that we hoped, with God's grace, to live out the best we could.

Bob had approached me a few days earlier.

"Honey, I can't believe at my age I'm even saying this . . . but I'm actually feeling nervous about the wedding night. I feel like a teenager who, quite frankly, doesn't know what the hell he is supposed to be doing!"

We both laughed. It was sweet and innocent. I was struck by the fact that taking a path of purity can actually restore something of original innocence and goodness even after a life of sexual disorder and promiscuity.

I was nervous too, but I said, "Oh, I'm sure you will know *exactly* what to do, my darling." I laughed and kissed him tenderly.

After the ceremony, we came home, and all sat around a beautiful outdoor patio listening to music, drinking champagne, and eating red velvet wedding cake with marzipan filling. Later came the expensive single malt Scotch, and the men smoking fat Cuban cigars. Most women hate the smoke and the smell, but since my beloved father was a cigar smoker, I love the aroma and happily breathed it in like church incense.

Bob said that was one of the reasons he married me.

Consummation

Like so many other couples, on our wedding night, we were exhausted from celebrating and we plopped into bed and fell asleep. But the next day, we took off for an elegant resort in the beautiful rolling vineyards of Napa Valley where we spent three days alone. We drank in the beauty of creation and expressed our wedding vows in body language. It was exciting, scary, and came with the same awkwardness we all face when things are new.

Romance leads to the Wedding Banquet

Heaven is described as the great, eternal wedding feast with juicy choice meats and rich aged wine (see Is 25:6) and intoxicating drink in such abundance that the very hills will run with wine (see Jl 3:18).

This wedding imagery is all throughout the Old and New Testaments; *"The kingdom of heaven may be compared to a king who gave a marriage feast for his son"* (Mt 22:2). In the book of Revelation, the apostle John has an astounding and mysterious vision of heaven as the marriage supper of the Lamb (see Rv 19:6–9).

Wine is one of those delicious goods that contain a hidden message and can point us to supernatural truth.

Do you remember the Gospel story of the wedding feast at Cana (see Jn 2:1–12)? In Jewish tradition, it was the responsibility of the bridegroom to provide the wine for the marriage supper. When the biblical bridegroom ran out of wine, Jesus the True Bridegroom came to his rescue and provided the best wine—wine that allowed everyone to drink to his or her fill and still have much left over. Among biblical scholars, wine has symbolized God's rich, intoxicating love. Adam, the first bridegroom, ran out of love. When we fail to love God as we should, we all run out of "wine." Jesus the Bridegroom comes to restore us all, to fill our hearts to full and over-flowing with the best and most abundant love. He was fulfilling the Old Testament prophecies of coming to marry his people—a marriage that eventually would be consummated on the cross.

And here we were . . . my new husband and I in California's famous Napa Valley, where the hills literally do run with wine! Aware of the rich spiritual symbolism of marriage—especially the eternal wedding feast to which we are all called—Bob and I arranged for an elaborate feast of our own.

At the gorgeous hillside resort of *L'auberge du Soleil*, we spent one late afternoon into the evening in a romantic outdoor gazebo among the vineyards. We were surrounded with vases of fresh-cut flowers and glowing candles all around. Over a four-hour period, our personal servers leisurely delivered an extravagant ten-course meal with wine pairings and decadent desserts—all to gentle strains of classical music and the setting sun.

It truly was a little taste of heaven right here on earth!

Marriage is unique. From the life and graces

that flow between Jesus and the Church, couples can drink abundantly and be filled with "new wine." Three other important insights will help you better understand God's great and tender love for us:

1. The wine Jesus provided was far better than what the wedding party had served. *God's ways are always best!*

2. The wine satisfied everyone to the full and there was still a lot left over. *God's ways are most abundant!*

3. The wine came out of the ritual cleansing jars where filthy hands were washed. If we empty ourselves to him, *God will purify our past and bring forth intoxicating love from our unclean hearts.*

Generation

I was far past child-bearing age when I married Bob, but new life sprang forth out of both our hearts. Bob blessed me with three step-sons, each of whom have continued to fill my mother's heart with the usual mix of worry, joy, and laughter. New hope, new dreams, and new graces filled us with a quiet happiness. Did we still have struggles to face and problems to overcome? Oh, yeah. But a new spirit of unity began to sink its roots deep into our lives.

Transformation

Shortly after we were married, Bob made it quite clear (several times) that I didn't squeeze out the kitchen sponge the right way. I repeatedly reminded him that he set the air conditioner at the wrong temperature. We were still discovering each other and both of us were afraid to be controlled, used, hurt, or otherwise not loved. Old emotional habits die hard and need supernatural graces to be purified. But at least we did agree on which way the toilet paper should roll!

Like any couple, we kept uncovering differences and had our ups and downs. But we were both determined to put them in their proper place to meet life together head on: there were bills to pay, young men to raise, work to do, and authentic, self-giving love to be forged. And, yes, we were smart enough to go to marriage counseling a few times to sort through things.

Marriage should get you to heaven

As young Catholic women, most of us learned that we had to help our spouse get to heaven. No one ever really reminded us that our spouse had the same job!

Marriage is meant to expose the attachments we have so that we can freely choose to let go for the greater good. It's where selfishness is exposed and deconstructed; it's where holiness grows. If that happens, true love blossoms and the marriage bond strengthens. Count on it: there will be times of maybe unimaginable sorrow, fear, and loneliness. There will be anger and there will be tears. But there will also be laughter and lovemaking.

The same thing is true of our interior marriage with the Lord.

Marriage is a holy communion

Life is difficult, and many times we struggle with feeling or even believing that we are loved. In marriage, we are supposed to be caught up into the divine exchange of love between the Persons of the Trinity and share in that most Holy Communion *so that we can pour that love like honey onto our spouse.*

Marriage has two particularly beautiful fruits:

1. to make visible and tangible to your spouse the incredibly merciful, tender, and extravagant love of God, and by this,
2. to help make your spouse experience his or her own goodness through your love.

Marriage should result in one spouse saying to the other, "Because of you, I know something of who God is and how much I am loved by him."

It takes prayer.

It takes grace.

It takes time.

It takes two.

And sometimes, it takes a lovely bottle of lush California cabernet.

Reflections

- What has gotten you through the tough times in your marriage?
- How do you feel when someone else prepares a fancy meal for you?
- With money as no object, describe the most luscious feast you would prepare for your spouse.

PART 3

About the Mass

If angels could be jealous of men, they would be so for one reason: Holy Communion.

—St. Maximillian Kolbe

18

Unveiling the Marriage in the Mass

The lifting of the veil of a virgin bride took place immediately before the marriage was consummated in sexual union. [The book of] Revelation unveils that bride. The climax of the Apocalypse, then, is the communion of the Church and Christ: the marriage supper of the Lamb.[24]

—Scott Hahn

D id you know that there is a marriage hidden in the Mass?

If in the "holy communion" of husband and wife, we see a little glimmer of the Holy

---

[24] Scott Hahn, *The Lamb's Supper* (New York: Doubleday, 1999).

Communion of Jesus and the Church, it should come as no surprise to discover the nuptial dimension of the Mass.

Most Catholics know the Mass is a sacrifice, but who is sacrificing for whom? *The Bridegroom for the Bride*.

You know the Mass is a meal, but what kind of a meal?

The wedding feast of the Lamb and the Bride.

Marriage and the Mass go hand in hand.

Wise old men know about love

In my youthful arrogance and ignorance, I once thought that priests, bishops, and popes were "old celibate men in Rome" who knew nothing about love, passion, and romance. How wrong I was!

Cardinal Raymond Burke is a strong proponent for beautiful and profoundly sacred liturgy. He's one of my favorites and among the most beloved clergy (and, sadly, most reviled) in our time, and he gets what is happening on that altar! He said, "The beauty of married life is in a very particular way perceived and confirmed in the Eucharistic Sacrifice."[25]

St. John Paul II, a perpetual student of human desire and expert on authentic love, called the Mass the sacrament of the Bride and Bridegroom. He said, "There is a marriage that leads to earthly life, consummated when husband and wife become 'one flesh.' And there is a marriage that leads to eternal life, consummated in the Eucharist" (*Mulieris Dignitatem*, 26).

J. R. R. Tolkien, Catholic author of the classic *Lord of the Rings*, said, "Out of the darkness of my life, so much frustrated, I put before you the one great thing to love on earth: the Blessed Sacrament. There you will find romance, glory, honour, fidelity, and the true way of all your loves on earth, and more than that: Death."[26]

A lot of people—even Catholics—are still

[25]   Jeanne Smits, "Exclusive interview: Cardinal Burke says confusion spreading among Catholics 'in an alarming way,'" *LifeSiteNews*, March 24, 2015, https://www.lifesitenews.com/news/exclusive-interview-cardinal-burke-says-confusion-spreading-among-catholics.

[26]   Peter Kreeft, *The Philosophy of Tolkien: The Worldview Behind the Lord of the Rings* (San Francisco: Ignatius, 2005), p. 219.

confused about what the Mass really is and what it means. Let's recall what we know.

The Mass is not just a mere community meal

Reducing the Mass to a family meal can strip it of its deeper meaning of a painful sacrifice. It's too often celebrated as if it were a mere parish potluck. Even the word *celebrate*—which we tend to equate with birthday parties or national holidays—can cause us to ignore its breathtaking reality.

It's not a stage presentation

It's not a liturgical parade, talent show, or a faith rally. It is not about the music, the homily, or the decorations, and yet all of those should point back to the central focus: Christ who surrenders himself to death, doing what the Bride could never do for herself.

The Mass is not the invention of man; it is a work of God

The Mass is the Bridegroom's movement toward us, his Bride, his sacrifice for our good, and our invitation to join him in his saving work. We are there, in his heart and at the cross, but we are not the center. He is.

Mass is the ultimate expression of love

The players are not the priest or even the people in the pews but Jesus Christ coming to the Father on our behalf, laying his life down on the cross to rescue us from the clutches of sin and death. The priest acts *in persona Christi* (in the person of Christ), but also even more beautifully *in persona Christi coniugis* (in the person of Christ, the Bridegroom) as we are individually and collectively his Bride.

The Mass is the same, one-time, sacrifice made present once again

It is not us trying to crucify Jesus again and again. It is his one, perfect, and eternal act of love that again opens to us, and into which we can frequently and mysteriously enter.

At Mass, we go to heaven

We move beyond the world's barriers into the invisible realm! The veil is lifted between heaven and earth and all the angels and saints join in perpetual worship of the Slain Lamb—the Bridegroom who gave his life for the Bride.

At Mass, Jesus consummates a marriage

We are invited to join in, to offer ourselves with Jesus to the Father, to be blessed and broken and poured out, and to (as yet) imperfectly consummate our mystical marriage with him, by opening like a bride and receiving him into our bodies. At Mass, God continues his pledge of love and we renew our vows.

In starkly marital language, Fulton Sheen said this:

> Who is our Lord on the cross? He's the new Adam. Where's the new Eve? At the foot of the cross. . . . If Eve became the

mother of the living in the natural order, is not this woman at the foot of the cross to become another mother? And so, the bridegroom looks down at the bride. He looks at his beloved. Christ looks at his Church. There is here the birth of the Church. As St. Augustine puts it, and here I am quoting him verbatim, "The heavenly bridegroom left the heavenly chambers, with the presage of the nuptials before him. He came to the marriage bed of the cross, a bed not of pleasure, but of pain, united himself with the woman, and consummated the union forever. As it were, the blood and water that came from the side of Christ was the spiritual seminal fluid." And so, from these nuptials "Woman, there's your son" this is the beginning of the Church.[27]

Cardinal Robert Sarah reminded the world at the 2016 Sacra Liturgia Conference in London, "The Liturgy is not about you and me;

---

[27]   Henry Dieterich, *Through the Year with Fulton Sheen* (San Francisco: Ignatius Press, 2003).

the Liturgy is first and foremost about God and what he has done for us."

Reflections

- Have you ever been bored at Mass? Why?
- Have you ever thought of a marriage being consummated at Mass?
- Why do you think some people might have difficulty with this imagery?

19

Consummating the Marriage

If we could comprehend all the good things contained in Holy Communion, nothing more would be wanting to content the heart of man.[28]

—St. John Vianney

Have you ever really noticed what happens at the very beginning of every Mass—even before a word is uttered?

The priest bows profoundly and kisses the altar.

This kiss is a sign of something beautiful, something profound, and, in a sense, something romantic! The priest venerates with special

---

[28]   St. Jean-Marie Vianney, *Sermons of the Cure of Ars* (New York: KIC Publishing, 1996).

honor and even affection the altar where Jesus empties himself out of love for his Bride. For me and for you.

The words and actions in the Mass are richly imbued with meaning, and if we really comprehended what was happening, we would weep uncontrollably with joy. As the stone in a diamond wedding ring has many facets, the Mass throws off many shining truths about God's love for us. I hope you will read with great happiness how this divine romance is brilliantly reflected in the nuptial dimension of the Mass.

Part 1: Liturgy of the Word

*God woos us with words of love
and life, and we respond.*

Invitation

Entrance greeting

The priest kisses the altar and invites us into the mystery.

Preparation

Penitential Act/Kyrie

As a bride, we prepare our minds and hearts to be united with him. We are rejecting sin, inordinate attachment, and anything that keeps us from total surrender to his love in the encounter we are about to have.

Communication

Gloria * Collect * Readings and Responsorial Psalm * Gospel

We adore him. We listen to him. We respond from our hearts to him.

The Gospel is God's message of love and hope and is the pinnacle of this first part of the Mass. We don't have to wait for the Holy Eucharist for Jesus as he is already truly with us in his Word. Imagine how truly present a husband is to his wife as he speaks words of love to her over dinner, perhaps, lovingly listening to her responses, and they enter into a dialogue of love. Later that night, he will still be fully present to her, but in an even more intimate way when he gives himself completely to her. His words prepare her heart for his body.

The priest (or deacon) kisses the book.

Homily

He speaks from his heart to us, his Beloved. Father Donald Calloway, MIC, posted a powerful reference to the marriage in the Mass on Facebook.

> When a priest or deacon preaches a homily, he is acting "in persona Christi coniugis" (in the person of Christ the bridegroom) and delivering the word (the seed of truth) to the bridal church. This is part of the reason why only ordained men give homilies. This is also why if a priest puts a barrier between himself and the faithful during the homily (that is, he holds back and doesn't give the bridal church the fullness of the seed through orthodox preaching) he is culpable of a form of spiritual contraception. Sure, a woman may be able to give a good speech, but it will never be a homily. Homilies

are reserved to ordained men who stand in the person of Christ the bridegroom. End of discussion.[29]

Creed

We stand. In the marital imagery, you could say this is where we accept God's proposal, saying yes to all that God and his Church propose for our belief. This ends the first part of the Mass— the Liturgy of the Word.

Remember, the validity of the Mass never rests on how we feel or even if we experience any sense of the transcendent. Reciting the Creed is both our private and public consent to the truth of our faith. The next time at Mass when you say the Creed, be aware that you are not simply agreeing with a check list of beliefs, but you are entrusting more and more of your life to God. *You are getting ready to renew "marriage" vows.*

---

[29]   Donald Calloway, Facebook post, March 3, 2016.

Part 2: Liturgy of the Eucharist

*The word God has spoken, and those we
have responded with, become flesh.*

Presentation

Presentation of the Gifts

The dialogue between Christ and the Bride shifts
now to a more somber and silent mood—something different and profound is about to happen.
In a pledge of unimaginable love, he offers himself to the Father and goes to the cross for us.
We cannot stop it, we abhor it, and yet we are so
thankful that he loved us so! The altar is a bed of
nuptial sacrifice. We offer ourselves in return to
him, and just as the bread and wine are changed,
so are we too, who surrender to become one
with him.

Consummation

Holy Communion

Jesus became the sacrifice to the Father that
we could not offer on our own. In giving his

body, he was crushed out of sheer love for us. We utterly adore him for this, and we keep our eyes on him as he is lifted up for all to see. We are not worthy of such love, but—knowing he has espoused himself to us—we are *made* worthy through him, in him, and with him. This brings us to our knees! In receiving him, we remain distinct but intertwined, our wills confirmed to his, and we are never so close to him in this life as we are at this moment.

Regarding the Eucharist, St. John Vianney said, "Upon receiving Holy Communion, the Adorable Blood of Jesus Christ really flows in our veins and his flesh is really blended with ours." St. Peter Chrysologus wrote, "He is The Bread sown in the virgin, leavened in the Flesh, molded in His Passion, baked in the furnace of the Sepulchre, placed in the Churches, and set upon the Altars, which daily supplies Heavenly Food to the faithful." Pope St. Leo the Great wrote, "By Holy Communion we are changed into the flesh of him who became our flesh."[30] And St. Pio of Pietrelcina said:

---

[30]   Pope Leo XIII, Encyclical *Mirae Caritatis*, May 28, 1902.

My heart feels as if it were being drawn by a superior force each morning just before uniting with Him in the Blessed Sacrament. I have such a thirst and hunger before receiving Him that it's a wonder I don't die of anxiety. I was hardly able to reach the Divine Prisoner in order to celebrate Mass. When Mass ended, I remained with Jesus to render Him thanks. My thirst and hunger do not diminish after I have received Him in the Blessed Sacrament, but rather, increase steadily. Oh, how sweet was the conversation I held with paradise this morning. The heart of Jesus and my own, if you will pardon my expression, fused. They were no longer two hearts beating but only one. My heart disappeared as if it were a drop in the ocean.[31]

---

[31]   Joseph Langford, *Mother Teresa's Secret Fire* (Huntington: Our Sunday Visitor, 2008).

Generation

Prayers after Communion

How can you not help but reflect on the wonder and miracle of what has just happened? It's not a time for chatter but a peaceful and sweet silence. Sometimes after Communion we will quietly or softly recite a short Psalm, words of praise to the God who loves us. Perhaps as a spouse prays that his wife will bear new life, the priest prays for the fruits of the mystery just celebrated. After such an intimate encounter with God, new divine life springs up in us! His seminal seeds of love will take root and grow in our hearts when we are rightly disposed. "He who eats my flesh and drinks my blood has eternal life" (Jn 6:54).

Transformation

Dismissal

Hopefully, when Mass is over, you have been changed. The weights and worries of the world you brought in are either gone or lighter. Your focus is less on you than on his love for you. And I am sure that overflow of his love pours out on all the people in the parking lot at whom you smile and gesture to go ahead of you!

The Mass never really ends. We are constantly being called by him to come away and renew our vows, to be filled with love, to be transformed, and then to go back out to change the world. It's the rhythm of our interior life and the days and nights of our mystical marriage. And I hope you will also take delight in noticing what happens at the end of every Mass: *The priest again bows profoundly and kisses the altar.*

Three kisses . . . two at the altar, one at the ambo. Look for them next time.

Reflections

- How do you feel about more intentionally entering the Mass as the Bride?
- What part of the Mass stirs up the greatest response in you?
- Do you think you could now explain this marital dimension to your children?

20

Living Happily Ever After

*The voice of the Spouse, that is, His inspiration,
in no way disturbs or troubles her, but draws her
so gently that He causes her soul to melt with delight and, as it were, to flow in to Him.*[32]

—St. Francis de Sales

I love to tell the story of my mother who one
night was frazzled down to nothing with her
rambunctious children, the endless piles of laun-
dry, the ever-mounting bills, and the dinner that
needed making. She stood resolutely at the stove
stirring the large pot of ham-hocks and beans
and holding a baby on her hip.

I approached to show her the "A" I had gotten

---

[32] Francis de Sales, *Finding Gods Will for You* (Man-
chester: Sophia Institute Press, 1998).

on my schoolwork that day—hoping for motherly attention, affection, and accolades. Instead, she ignored it and shoved the baby into my arms.

"Take your brother and change him," and she gruffly ordered me to clear the table, set it, and call the other kids inside to wash for supper.

Okay, then. Mom was having a bad day.

A short while later. Dad came home, and everyone was excited to see him. But after he patted all our little heads, he made his way straight for Mom and gave her a big kiss on the lips. He opened the liquor cabinet and poured two short Scotches and handed one to Mom.

I watched as they talked, and Mom began to laugh a little. Dad kissed her again, hugged her, and lovingly patted her on the behind. I loved them loving each other.

I didn't notice until a little while later that they . . . were gone. The beans were still simmering and, as I peered up the stairs, I saw their bedroom door was shut. What were they doing? About half an hour later, when Mom emerged from their room, she was completely changed. A peaceful, contented glow radiated from her and she smiled at me with her eyes.

"Sugar Pie," she said in a sing-song voice, "Show me your schoolwork again."

Her face was slightly flushed, and she was soft and warm and sweet.

I grabbed my paper and ran up close to her.

"*Very* nice, honey." She paused, pulled me into her, and kissed the top of my head.

Then she put her hand gently on my chin and lifted my face to look into it.

"Rosie, thank you for being my good girl. You're a good big sister. You're such a help around the house and I don't know what I would do without you!"

She squeezed me again.

Before Dad came home, Mom had been emptied and had almost nothing to give. When he arrived and began to sweet-talk her, she was reminded it was time to leave her work and her children—two things we women think are most important—for something even more essential: to be alone with her spouse and renew their love. From the overflow of Dad's love, Mom was able to pour her maternal love out on her children like rich, thick, orange-blossom scented honey.

In the interior life, there are times when the

soul will feel spiritually dry, and much of that is natural and no cause for alarm. Sometimes, it is even necessary to help purify us from unnecessary attachments. But always, in at least an act of the will, we can "leave" what is weighing us down and go be alone with him. We can do what saints have called "the practice of the presence of God."[33]

Some of us are runaway brides

To commit to another person is to embark on a very challenging journey. To commit to the Almighty God is even more adventurous! We intuitively know that God wants all of us. We know that we have to be willing to come apart at the seams, to be dismantled, to let our ego fall apart before we can begin to become the person God created us to be. To be made ready for intimate union with God, we have to allow him access to those secret, untested, messy parts of ourselves so that he can change us. That's scary.

---

[33]   Brother Lawrence, *The Practice of the Presence of God* (New Kensington, PA: Whitaker House, 1982).

And it makes a lot of us *run*.

But the more we run, the more the mess will fester. Eventually we will become terrified of commitment and find ways to justify it.

Why would a good God permit such horrible evil?

Why did God not answer my prayer?

Why can't I hear God?

This is a vicious circle that keeps us cut off from and afraid of God and ourselves. We are operating from the raw wound of our heart: feeling disconnected from our true nature as his beloved and not trusting that he really loves us. And *that* is a lie from the pit of hell. We must pray—even if we don't believe it or feel it—for God to woo us back to himself.

Some have avoided the bridal chamber

Another way of fleeing from God is what I call "spiritual simulation," where the soul lives in a close relationship with God but never offers or receives the fullness of that relationship. To feel "married to God," one can immerse herself in spiritual practices and church-speak and still avoid the intimacy of total surrender of her heart. Ultimately out of fear and distrust, she lives in a constant state of bypassing the challenging work of total transformation. Why?

Because everything changes behind closed doors.

My elderly friend Sharon shook her head and just laughed when she recalled her honeymoon some fifty years earlier.

"I was so scared! I didn't want him to see me naked. I tried everything to make sure he couldn't see the flaws."

She rolled her eyes in recollection and laughed again.

"Rose, I hid in the bathroom as long as I could until it was time to come out. I ran into bed and pulled my nightgown tight around me. When he started kissing me, I just pulled it tighter. I didn't know what the heck I was doing. God, I was naïve. Poor guy."

If the soul has been safeguarding her deep, interior self from God or anyone else probing too deeply, it's probably because of her past experiences and fears. She's afraid to be looked at, critically assessed, and judged not worthy. Or maybe afraid to lose some form of identity, security, or pleasure to which she's attached. She's afraid of discomfort or pain. It is a natural and even good reaction for a woman to close the most intimate parts of herself off from those she believes may hurt or abuse her. In that, she is "protecting the gift" of her goodness. That which is most sacred is often beautifully veiled, kept partially hidden and unattainable until the right time with the right person.

But you and I were not made to live behind the veil. The self-protective mechanisms of our hearts can also act as obstructive barriers between us and the Love who wants to tenderly possess us—all of us.

Don't be ashamed of fear; surrender it to God.

Some of us need a new heart

Little Camila had a weakened, stiffened heart muscle, a condition called restrictive cardiomy-opathy. Doctors decided to give her a second heart, often called a "piggyback" heart transplant. The new heart is grafted onto the old so that they begin to work together even though each maintains its own separate rhythm. Over time, if the old heart fails, the new one will eventually take over.

What a powerful image of the invisible surgery God can do for us by grafting his Sacred Heart to ours! Little Camila's heart had a hardened muscle. Sometimes we call people who have lost hope, joy, and the ability to respond to love as being hard-hearted or having a heart of stone. Our desire for a true and faithful love, even if rationalized away, or relegated to the dark recesses of forgotten memories, points to our very reason for being. It never goes away. It may have shrunk down to the size of a shriveled pea at the back of an old pantry shelf. But God will find your heart and graft it to his own. There are many stories of saints and mystics who have exchanged hearts with Jesus.

"A new heart I will give you, and a new spirit I will put within you; and I will take out of your flesh the heart of stone and give you a heart of flesh" (Ez 36:26).

Some of us have been unfaithful

There are lots of forms of infidelity in marriage.

Even on the worst days when I felt angry or trapped in marriage, I'd never even thought of being with another man. But God broke through that pride when I realized all the other ways I had been unfaithful:

- trying to wear the proverbial pants,
- making my job more important than him,
- putting my ministry over his needs,
- giving first fruit of affection and loyalty due my spouse to the children,
- putting him down to others,
- making him the object of supposed marital jokes,
- making major decisions and telling him afterward,
- expecting him to not stand in the way of things I wanted,
- and spending inordinate time with others before time with him.

We can do all these things in our relationship with God.

Some are simply distracted

The soul can have freely surrendered her heart to God but then find herself tired, distracted, or simply worn down by the gravity of life. What does she need to do? Renew her wedding vows. Maybe you just need to do what my mom did: leave the dinner, the kids, all your work and worries, and go spend some alone time with him, opening to him, and allowing him to pull you into his very heart to fill you up to overflowing with his love. You don't need to ask God to be patient with you. He already is. He wants to take your warm affection for him and ignite it to a burning love affair.

In his *Confessions*, St, Augustine said, "Go on, O Lord, and act: stir us up and call us back; inflame us and draw us to thee; stir us up and grow sweet to us; let us now love thee, let us run to thee."[34]

---

[34]   St. Augustine, *Confessions*, bk. 8, ch. IV, no. 9.

After every wedding comes a marriage

In the interior life, our relationship with Christ will also pass through the honeymoon stage and move into the day-to-day hammering out of true love. But traces of the honeymoon memories will always reappear—like they did in my mom's "magic suitcase."

I was thrilled the first time I was invited to spend the night at a friend's house. I had never stayed away on my own and needed an overnight bag. After school, I gathered up my toothbrush, barrettes, pajamas, and some play clothes for the next day and asked Mom if I could use a piece of her luggage. She went to her closet and pulled out a small vintage suitcase with brass hinges and a tweed fabric exterior. It opened to reveal satin fabric lining and pockets.

"I first used this on my honeymoon, Rosie," Mom told me.

Wow, I thought, *that was so long ago.* I'd often seen my mother use the suitcase when she and Dad went away for a weekend to San Francisco, which they did often. I wanted to know more about her wedding and the celebration afterward.

She pulled some of the fabric away from the inside and announced, "Yes! There it is!"

Plucking a few grains of old rice out of the lining, Mom explained that this was a very special suitcase. She told me what fun they had on their honeymoon, how romantic it was, and that it was so enchanting that some of that magic was still in the suitcase. After marrying Dad, no matter how many times she shook, pulled, poked, and vacuumed, rice that had been thrown at her wedding and had been in her clothes would mysteriously appear for years.

"I think it's God's way of telling us to always remember the magic of our honeymoon." I believed her, and for many years when I used it, I would look for—and find—a few rice kernels.

Romance will bring wounds of love

A modern popular put-down of the trials of marriage goes like this:

First comes the engagement ring.

Then comes the wedding ring.

Then comes the suffer-ring.

You either will or already have had a honeymoon experience with God. Enjoy those moments, but understand they are not meant to last. Our Lord wants to prepare you to be with him in the battlefield to continue his saving work in the world. There will be what the saints call "dark nights" and "desolations" which are times of spiritual dryness.

Most people understand the struggles of uniting two imperfect souls in an earthly marriage. Suffering is part of purification; every marriage requires sacrifice—the actual living out of the vows. The special spiritual favors which God chooses to bestow on some saints are often referred to as wounds of love.

But those don't last, either. Don't be discouraged.

Keep your eyes and heart open for the reminders of his love and the intimacy you have together, even when you can't always feel it.

Just keep looking for the rice.

Reflections

- How have these reflections changed you?
- What do you think God is saying to you?
- What would you like to say to God?

Conclusion

*Keep tight inside of them. Their mag-
ic must be very powerful.*[35]

—Glinda, the Good Witch of the North

After reading this book, I hope you will look
down and see you have been wearing your
own pair of sparkling ruby slippers all along.
They were given to you at your baptism when
you were espoused to the Bridegroom—and
their "magic" (the graces that flow from the Sacrament) is very powerful. When the tornadoes
of fear or self-doubt blow away your interior
peace, just click your heels together, three times,
and say:

There's no *love like his.*
There's no *love like his.*

---

[35]   *Wizard of Oz*, 1939.

There's no *love like his.*

You'll be immediately transported to your real home—inside the heart of God—and you can go there any time. Better yet, he beckons you to the most special intimacy with him this side of heaven in the Holy Sacrifice of the Mass, where he continually offers you his Body, Blood, Soul, Divinity—and all of his heart. At Mass, you will hear Scripture that is his love letter to you— promises to give you the happiness you desire.

Whenever you need to remember, take the following letter out and read it.

God's Love Letter to You

I love you so much! (see Jn 3:16). Even when you don't feel it, believe it, or fully trust it.

I have loved you from the very beginning and always will (see 1 Jn 4:19).

You are my precious daughter (see 1 Jn 3:1), *created in my image* (see Gn 1:27). I look upon you with such tenderness and I see you are "very good" (Gn 1:31).

I knew you even before you were born, and I desired you (see Ps 139:13).

You are never out of or far away from my thoughts, which are as countless as the sand on the seashore (see Ps 139:17–18).

I know everything about you, and you will always delight me! (see Ps 18:19).

I see and love all of you! I know the number of the hairs on your head (see Mt 10:30), and I am familiar with all your ways (see Ps 139:3).

I am the perfect Father who knows how to love you the way you deeply desire. (see Mt 5:48) No matter your fatherly wounds, I can give you more than he ever could (see Mt 7:9–11).

I love to lavish good things on you (see Mt 7:11).

I am for you and not against you! (see Rom 8:31).

I will fight for you when enemies come against you (see Ps 44:7).

I see your goodness and will bless you even when others insult and mistreat you (see Mt 5:11).

I will raise you up when you trust me and wait for my timing (see Mt 23:12).

Your own parents or family may forsake you, but I never will (see Ps 27:10).

I will quiet your troubled mind. When you're

overwhelmed or discouraged, I will be there for you to help you and give you rest (see Zep 3:17).

I'll comfort you in your time of sadness (see Mt 5:4).

When you are brokenhearted, I will draw very close to you (see Ps 34:18) and mourn with you (see Jn 11:35).

When you weep, I'll collect all your tears in my bottle and record each one in my book (see Ps 56:8).

Just as I look after the little sparrow, so will I look after you (see Mt 10:26–31).

You're never alone; bring your heavy burdens to me and I will help you carry them (see Mt 11:28–30).

Talk to me when you're anxious and let me put you at peace (see Phil 4:6).

I'll carry you tenderly, and close to my heart— like a shepherd with his lamb (see Is 40:11).

I will give you rest (see Mt 11:28).

I'll turn your mourning into gladness (see Jer 31:13) and your weakness into strength (see 2 Cor 12:9–10).

I'll be your safeguard when the world is falling apart. When rivers of difficulty roar, you will not be swept away. When fiery trials blaze, you will

not be burned (see Is 43:2). When war breaks
out, I will be your place of safety, an ever-present
help in trouble (see Ps 46). Even when you face
death, I will take you by the hand and lead you
on the joyful path to eternal life (see Ps 16:9–11).

I will put a joyful new song in your mouth (see
Ps 40:3) and give you a beautiful new name (see
Is 62:2).

I want to give you a future filled with hope! (see
Jer 29:11).

*I want to give you not just life but abundant life,
overflowing with goodness!* (see Jn 10:10). Now
and always (see Jn 3:36).

*I am compassionate and gracious, slow to anger
and rich in mercy,* and abounding in love and
faithfulness (see Ex 34:6).

*I long for all your love and I knock on the door
of your heart,* waiting for you to let me in (see
Rv 3:20).

Open the door and I will forgive your sins (see
Acts 10:43) and remember them no more (see
Is 43:25).

*Don't be afraid, my love; if you rely on me, then
my perfect love will remove all of your fear* (see 1
Jn 4:18).

If you have been crushed, I will give you a new heart (see Ez 36:26), a new self (see Eph 4:24), and a new life (see Rom 6:4).

I will teach you how to live to be truly happy (see Mt 4:17).

I will fill you to overflowing with my Holy Spirit (see Jn 3:3)

I will make your goodness and beauty shine like the dawn (see Ps 37:6).

You will be a crown of glory in my hand (see Is 62:3), reflecting my likeness with ever-increasing beauty (see 2 Cor 4:18).

I will purify you and make you beautiful and holy (see 1 Thes 5:24) and bring to completion the good work I've started in you (see Phil 1:6).

I will give you love, joy, peace, and all the fruits of my Spirit to fill your mind, heart, and soul (see Gal 5:22–23).

Know that when you love me and seek my purposes that all things will work together for your good (see Rom 8:28).

Don't turn away; come to me (see Jas 4:7); turn away from sin and toward the goodness I will give you (see Rom 12:21).

Call out for me and I will always hear and answer you (see Jer 33:3).

You're safe with me (see Jn 10:28). Like a mother bird, I'll protect and cover you with my feathers in my nest (see Ps 91:1–4).

I can and will do much more for you than you can ever imagine (see Eph 3:20).

I, who made you, am your Beloved Bridegroom; I long for you to be my bride (see Is 54:5).

I desire you and delight in you even more than a bridegroom for his bride (see Is 62:5). Will you marry me? Will you give me your all?

You have been betrothed to me as my beloved (see 2 Cor 11:2); now will you enter the bridal chamber?

I want you to work alongside me in my work of bringing love to the world (see Hg 2:4).

Together we can change the world (see Mk 10:27) and move mountains! (see Mt 17:20).

Desire me more than anything else and I will give you the deep desires of your heart (see Ps 37:4)

I will never leave you, my precious one (see Heb 13:5).

I will always, always, always, love you! (see Jer

31:3) and nothing can ever change that! (see Rom 8:38–39).

Will you say yes?

I pray for you, dear reader. Will you pray for me?